JOB HUNTING SECRETS &TACTICS

by Kirby W. Stanat with Patrick Reardon

Follett/Westwind

Text copyright ©1977, Kirby Stanat and Patrick Reardon
Illustration copyright ©1977, Westwind Press

Library of Congress Number: 76-49663

1 2 3 4 5 6 7 8 9 0 81 80 79 78 77

Printed in the United States of America.

Published by   Westwind Press
A Division of
Raintree Publishers Limited
Milwaukee, Wisconsin 53203

Distributed by   Follett Publishing Company
1010 West Washington Street
Chicago, Illinois 60607

Library of Congress Cataloging in Publication Data
Stanat, Kirby.
  Job hunting secrets and tactics.

  1. Vocational guidance. 2. Employment
interviewing. I. Reardon, Patrick, joint author.
II. Title.
HF5381.S737   6501.14   76-49663
ISBN 0-8172-0508-X
ISBN 0-8172-0509-8 lib. bdg.

II

Dedication

To Bink Stanat and Maureen Reardon.

Also to three capable secretaries: Verna Mae Fitzpatrick, Kathy Kulakowski and Louise Maxworthy.

Acknowledgments

I am deeply grateful to the following for their valuable contributions to this book:

The College Placement Council, Inc., for permission to reprint its copyrighted code, *Principles and Practices of College Career Planning, Placement, and Recruitment.*

Ruth Dugan, for permission to print her material on employment agencies.

Frank S. Endicott and Northwestern University and its Placement Center, for permission to reprint material from the Endicott Report, which is copyrighted by the university.

Harold Matson Company, Inc., for permission to quote from William Manchester's biography of H. L. Mencken, *Disturber of the Peace*, copyright, 1950, 1951 by William Manchester.

John T. Molloy, for permission to quote from his book, *Dress for Success,* copyright 1975, John T. Molloy.

To all of the recruiters and other personnel and placement people I have associated with over the years, many of whom provided helpful information for this book.

—Kirby W. Stanat

Table of Contents

IV

1

INTRODUCTION

Throw off your misconceptions about job hunting

Over the last 20 years I have watched hundreds of job applicants destroy themselves in the first few seconds of an interview. I have seen others, just seconds away from being hired, do things that ruined their chances.

Very few people are highly skilled at getting a job because job hunting isn't something most people do every day. It's a sometime skill that most people use only a few times in their lives.

Most job seekers do not understand the hiring process. They haven't thought it through. They don't understand its basic nature, let alone its subtleties. They do not know how to conform to its demands or how to take advantage of its weaknesses.

Misconceptions about the hiring process abound. A few basic ones deserve special attention.

• Job hunters think their qualifications will get them the job. They will not. Social workers are not hired for their ability to do social work; teachers are not hired for their teaching skill; computer programmers are not hired for their skill at programming computers; decision makers are not hired for their ability to make decisions.

• Job hunters too often think their lack of qualifications will keep them from getting the job. Frequently they should think again.

1

• Many people think their resume will get them the job. It will not. Resumes cause more people to be rejected than hired.

• Job hunters think they should follow instructions every step of the way. That can be a costly mistake.

• Job hunters think potential allies are adversaries and enemies are friends. They don't know who they should run with and who they should run over.

I have watched the hiring process run its course thousands of times — from every possible angle. I have been an applicant for about a dozen professional jobs, and, like other candidates, I have made mistakes.

I have hired people — about 8,000 of them. The first 13 years of my professional life were spent in industry as a personnel specialist and recruiter. I have hired floor sweepers and high-level managers. During the height of the aerospace industry boom in the 1960s, I hired hundreds of highly skilled technicians for a major aerospace manufacturer in Denver. I spent six years as chief recruiter for a large manufacturer of motors. I have hired people of every sex, color, religion, and lifestyle imaginable.

I am now a third party in the hiring process, a marriage broker between college students and employers. For the last seven years I have been placement director for the University of Wisconsin – Milwaukee, which has 25,000 students. My job is to help college-degree candidates find their first professional jobs and to help older, more experienced people change jobs.

I have watched in frustration as students have done unbelievable things during job interviews. And I have recoiled at some of the weird things I have seen recruiters do — things I unwittingly did when I was a recruiter. In the seven years I have held my job, I have constantly excoriated students for their blunders, and I have consistently chided recruiters for their way of doing things.

As placement director, my major function is teaching students how the hiring process works. And that is the thrust of this book: how the system works and how you can work it.

The background information, principles, and tactics in this book will be useful to anyone who is now or will be in the job market. Regardless of your age, your sex, your experience, your salary level, your goals, or the type of job you want, this book applies to you.

Recent high school graduates, college students, new college graduates, people who are looking for a different job, women who are reentering the job market after an absence of a few years, people who have been fired or laid off, all can take advantage of the tactics this book describes. The methods of getting the job interview will vary for these groups, but the interview itself will not.

Item A

Your chances in the job market are improved vastly when you understand what is happening — not what *seems* to be happening, but what is really going on.

There are several things you should know about when you look for a job:

• People

The people you will be dealing with: recruiters, department managers, receptionists, employment agency people.

How do they operate?

What pressures are they under?

What rewards do they get?

What do they like and dislike?

How can you manipulate them?

• Machinery

How does the hiring process work?

4

Who does what? When do they do it, and why?

• Power

Who has it and who doesn't?
How is it used?
When do you have power and when are you weak?
How can you use the power you have?

• Geography

What happens where?
Where do you have to be to get hired?
What is friendly soil for you and what is hostile terrain?

• Tools

When should you use the telephone and when should you avoid it?
When does your resume help you and when can it hurt you?

• Tactics

What works for you and what doesn't?
What tactics do the people on "the other side" use?

• Attitudes

How do the people you will be dealing with feel about things?
What should be your attitude throughout the hiring process?

THESE THINGS ARE WHAT THE REST OF THIS BOOK IS ABOUT.

THE RECRUITER

Learn who the recruiter is and why you have leverage over him

If you spend some time thinking about job interviews, you probably will consider only one dimension of what happens — your side.

You want to impress the recruiter and get a job. Even if you enjoy interviewing, you probably are a little nervous about it. The recruiter, that awesome individual who will pass judgment on you, seems to be an adversary with enormous power over your life, your destiny. And you, poor you, are a supplicant sitting there with no leverage.

If that's what you think, you're wrong. That line of thought contains myths that this chapter will annihilate.

In this chapter we will take a microscopic look at the recruiter and find out what makes this functionary spin and whir. Who is the recruiter? Exactly how much power does he or she have? What pressure is the recruiter under, and how can you take advantage of that pressure? How much power do *you* have?

Who Is the Recruiter?

Recruiter is the term most often used in business to describe the person who conducts the first interview you have with an organization. The recruiter could be:

• The personnel manager or director of industrial relations of a small or medium-sized company. His duties

6

often go far beyond hiring and may include such things as labor negotiations and employee policy.

• A subordinate in the personnel department whose major role is interviewing prospective employees. In big manufacturing companies, there often is a white collar recruiter, who interviews technical people, managers, salespersons, secretaries, and file clerks, and a blue collar recruiter, who interviews production workers.

• The manager of a department other than personnel. In some companies, department heads do the recruiting.

• A salesperson, engineer, nurse, teacher, or other specialist who does occasional interviewing of job candidates.

What Does the Recruiter Do?

In most large organizations the person who conducts the first interview with you is not the person who hires you. The hiring is done later, probably by the head of the department you will be working in.

The recruiter makes a *screening* decision. From the applicants he has interviewed, he picks out those people who seem best suited for the jobs open in his company. Then he sends his prizes back to the department head, who makes the hiring decision.

Recruiters interview job candidates in corporate offices or on the road. Some visit colleges and interview students at the campus placement center. A great deal of interviewing is done in motel rooms; some takes place in restaurants and bars.

What Sort of Character Is the Recruiter?

If you ask a recruiter what he likes most about his job, he probably will say, "I like working with people." Recruiters generally are outgoing and personable. Recruiting is an ideal job for an extrovert. But most recruiters aren't extroverted to the point of being backslappers and glad-handers. They tend to be more sophisticated.

Most recruiters are intelligent. Their work demands that they have an extraordinary perception of people and a grasp of what is required for different jobs.

They generally are conservative. Recruiters are show-cases for their organizations and reflect the solid, "sensible" image their organizations try to project.

This is about as far as the generalities go.

The recruiters you deal with may be men or women, young or old, contemporary or old-fashioned. Some are serious, no-nonsense characters, and a few are downright inscrutable.

How Good Are They?

Most recruiters are interesting and interested people, dedicated to doing a good job, so the odds are that you will be dealing with sharp people who know what they are doing. *But don't count on it.* There are some incompetents:

• Hardly a recruiting week goes by that most campus placement directors don't encounter a recruiter with a sledgehammer hangover that can be seen *and* smelled. I once had to wake a recruiter whose snores were disturbing the recruiter interviewing students in the next room.

• One engineer occasionally was sent out to recruit as a punishment. Whenever he got in hot water, his boss put him on the road to talk to job candidates. He hated traveling and despised recruiting, so he was in a rotten mood, and it was almost impossible for job seekers to make a good impression on him.

• One young recruiter interviewing on my campus seemed nervous. I got to talking with him and found out why. He had been working for a company in the Southwest for less than a week! He said the company had done him the favor of sending him on a recruiting junket to the Midwest so he could rendezvous with his fiancée in Michigan.

Newness to the company and lack of training are fairly common reasons for poor recruiting. But there are some veteran incompetents, too, poor recruiters who have been too stupid, too lazy, or too unobservant to learn their own company. They don't know an underwriter from an accountant, and they have failed to catch the signals from their department heads about what kinds of people they want working for them. Since these weak recruiters don't know what to look for in a job candidate, they might fill your interview time with talk about the weather.

A good recruiter knows the company well, understands the jobs that have to be filled, and knows what the company's department managers want. Some recruiters have their sensors so well honed that they can pick the right candidate out of a field of 50 almost every time.

Some companies make sure that every recruiter they have is a highly skilled, hand-picked pro. Some firms put new recruiters through a tough, two- or three-day seminar on interviewing, including what questions to ask — and why — and how to evaluate a candidate's responses. These sessions are followed by practice interviews observed by a senior recruiter. (Companies sometimes pay college students to be interviewees in dry runs.) For the first few real interviews, the new recruiter is teamed with a veteran. When it comes time to work alone, the recruiter is prepared.

A Corporate Weakling

In the corporate pecking order, the personnel manager usually has about as much status as a king's fool. Personnel is traditionally the weakest department in the organization, and personnel people are looked down on by top management because:

• They do not deal with customers.

• They do not handle cash or have company financial contacts.

• They do not touch the product.

That means they are pure overhead. When I was a personnel manager, there were times when I started to make suggestions in executive meetings only to have the company president cut me off with, "Aw, shut up, Overhead." The personnel department gets the limelight only during union negotiations or a strike.

Personnel is everybody's lackey. Line managers are fond of saying, "Hey, Recruiter, get hot. If we have to lay off, the guy who does the hiring will be the first to go. Ha-ha-ha." That's not what happens, but such comments don't do much for the personnel manager's feeling of security.

There are, however, some personnel people who, because of their strong personalities or skill at politicking, have cut themselves a slice of power within a company.

The Midwest recruiter for one major corporation, a former hotshot salesman, has considerable clout. He can move employees around, which is unusual. If the Tulsa office has an opening, he can snatch someone out of the Indianapolis office. Still, he doesn't have nearly as much internal influence as the Midwest sales manager.

Do you know of any vice-president of personnel or industrial relations being promoted to president? Probably not. There are a few, but not many. Presidents are chosen from the provinces of the corporate grandees — marketing, manufacturing, finance — not personnel.

At one huge accounting firm there are several hundred partners. Only two have ever come from personnel. So the chances are that this "awesome" figure who is interviewing you is no lion in his own organization.

If personnel is such a weak department and such a dead-end, why do people go into it and stay in it? Because

10

they get a "buzz" out of it. Recruiting can be fun. To have a department manager come back and tell you, "The new kid's really working out," is a booster shot in the ego.

But for every thrill there is a thud. One of the biggest letdowns comes when the recruiter has connected with "Supercandidate" and the department head blows it. Nearly every seasoned recruiter has a mate for these true stories:

A recruiter met a hot prospect on the college circuit a few years ago. He was an outstanding candidate. He was coming to town to interview with several companies, and they all wanted him. He wanted to go into sales, so the recruiter brought the candidate in for an interview with the sales manager...and the sales manager spent his interview hour not talking to the candidate, but talking to somebody on the phone! At the end of the day the candidate told the recruiter, "I enjoyed the tour through the plant. I enjoyed the luncheon and most of the people I met, but in my hour with the sales manager all I did was listen to him talk on the phone." The candidate took a job at another company.

The chief draftsman at one company needed some drafting people, but at the time, draftsmen were hard to find. The recruiter went out and broke his back looking for draftsmen. The chief draftsman stopped in the recruiter's office every morning to complain that he had fallen behind and needed people.

Finally the recruiter found a draftsman — a good one. The recruiter talked briefly with the candidate he had found and then set up an appointment in his own office for 9:00 the next morning. He also checked with the chief draftsman and made a 10:00 A.M. appointment for the candidate in the chief draftsman's office. The recruiter interviewed the candidate at 9:00. Then at 9:45, the recruiter went up to the chief draftsman's office to tell him about the candidate. The chief draftsman said, "Yeah, I know I have an appointment, but I'm too busy to see him today. Tell him to come back another time."

The stunned recruiter said, "Look, the guy took off work to come and see you."

The chief draftsman said, "I don't care. Tell him to come another day."

The company did not land that draftsman. The department head had blown it. And a few days later, sure enough, the chief draftsman came roaring back at the recruiter with a demand for more candidates.

The Recruiter and You...and the Pressure on the Recruiter

The recruiter suffers a lot of frustrations and is usually a weakling in corporate circles. When the recruiter is interviewing you for a job, however, he is loaded with power. But don't be overawed by it, for there are pressures that run counter to that power.

When the company needs new employees, the recruiter must come up with warm bodies. He can't go back to his boss and say, "Sorry, Boss, couldn't find anybody." The boss would say, "Sorry, Recruiter, I'll find somebody who can."

Because the recruiter needs people, you can manipulate him. He wants to be manipulated; he *has* to be manipulated by someone or he's in trouble. So while the recruiter may seem to be an adversary, that's only an illusion. He wants to find an ally, and all you have to do is demonstrate that you would be a worthy one.

And that is where the second pressure on the recruiter comes in.

Not only does the recruiter have to supply warm bodies, he must supply *good* warm bodies. In your job interviews your future isn't the only one on the line. The recruiter's is, too, and you can mean something to that future.

While the recruiter is a judge, he also must be judged. Remember, the recruiter usually doesn't do the hiring. He sends you to Charlie, the department head, and Charlie decides whether or not you will be hired.

That is where it gets sticky for the recruiter.

If he sends a steady parade of clods to Charlie, or if he sells Charlie on several people who don't work out, that recruiter is a good candidate to become a door-to-door magazine salesman. *The recruiter has to deliver quality.* He has to deliver people who are right for his company. And that is what he is thinking about when he is interviewing you. He is thinking about his company, with all of its intramural politics, peccadillos and corporate migraines. He is thinking about Charlie and all of Charlie's attitudes and prejudices. He's wondering how you will fit into all of that.

In any corporation, the new employee has an invisible sign around his or her neck for two or three years. What the sign says is, "Hired by Joe Recruiter."

When I was a recruiter, I was always conscious of the invisible signs on the people who were hired on the basis of my recommendation. I knew that I was being judged on their performance. If I tended to forget that, I got reminders:

A young engineer I hired straight out of college had been on the job about two months when he did something dumb. It must have been extraordinarily dumb because it caused a short that affected equipment outside the building, and half of a small town was without electricity for a while. I was the first guy they called. I was in another building, 15 miles away. "Hey, Kirby," said the voice on the other end of the phone, "do you know what your dumb kid just did?" My dumb kid! I wasn't the kid's boss. I hadn't seen him in 60 days. But I was the one who recommended that he be hired, so he was my dumb kid.

When something goes wrong, people have to have somebody to chew out, and when a new employee screws up, they will shove it down the recruiter's throat. Every new employee is a Sword of Damocles hanging over the recruiter's neck.

Your power in a job interview is directly proportionate to your ability to capitalize on the pressures on the recruiter. What you have to do is make it extremely difficult for that recruiter to reject you. You have to make him feel that he is not taking a risk by betting a portion of his corporate hide on you. To carry this point one step further, you have to make him feel that he *would* be taking a chance by passing you up in favor of someone else, someone who might not be as good as you. (Later chapters will show you how you can make it difficult for the recruiter to reject you.)

The Recruiter as Czar

Although the recruiter can be hung by his thumbs for recommending people who don't work out, there is one area in which he is a czar: the negative decision.

While the recruiter usually cannot hire you, he or she can reject you — with impunity. That makes the recruiter a judge whose decision is almost irreversible. His decisions are not overturned. Not all of the people he recommends are hired; those are merely *recommendations*. His rejections are *decisions*. And the people he turns away have practically no avenue of appeal within the company. Who would you talk to? The company president? The department head? In most cases, particularly in big organizations, that would be a waste of time. They don't want to talk to you: they aren't being paid to make screening decisions. The recruiter is.

So if, on the basis of a 20-minute interview, the recruiter decides you don't merit further consideration, you simply don't get any further consideration. You're in the discard pile, and no boss will land on the recruiter for turning you away, because superiors don't ask recruiters to justify negative decisions.

If the recruiter decides to reject you, he writes "Regret and file" on your application. Then his secretary sends you a form letter telling you, "Sorry, no job." Your application will be filed, cross-indexed in a couple of ways, and promptly forgotten. Six months later that file will be purged, and your application will hit the trash. You're gone. You've never talked to anybody but the recruiter. Nobody has questioned his decision. And if you were to send a follow-up letter to the president of the company asking what the hell ever happened to your application, the president would simply scrawl "Answer this" on it and send it down to the recruiter.

But there are exceptions. While most recruiters are almost omnipotent when making a negative decision, you should not expect that to be true in all cases. The system used by most big companies — a close screening by the recruiter with his recommendations sent on to the department head — is not universal. Sometimes you *will* be hired by the person who conducts the first interview with you. You could find yourself having your first interview with a large group from the organization. There are variations at every step in the hiring process, and you should be alert for them. You have to figure out just what's going on and then act on it. Here's an example:

A chain of clothing stores ran a help-wanted ad in a newspaper for an advertising manager. The ad listed the name of the personnel manager and asked applicants to send a resume to her. A woman who was interested in the job ignored the request for a mailed-in resume and went in the next day to see the personnel manager. She waited around for about two hours before the personnel manager returned to her office. The personnel manager came out into the lobby to give the woman a quick brush-off. The personnel manager told the woman that the company president was going to start interviewing only applicants with retail advertising experience.

The woman, who had strong credentials but no retail experience, read the situation: the personnel manager was not doing any face-to-face screening or making any intelligent judgments. She was merely opening letters and sending resumes to the president. No need to talk with the personnel manager anymore.

So the woman left, called the company president, and told him that "Ms. Brown (the personnel manager) said you were only interviewing candidates with retail experience. I don't have that, but I have exceptionally good credentials, and I'm right for the job." She gave him a brief summary of her qualifications, and the president was impressed by them. He also told her he was impressed by her aggressiveness. He asked her to come in an hour later for an interview. She went — and she got a job offer.

The Recruiter as Intelligence Agent...and as Prosecutor

If the recruiter is going to wager a piece of his career on you, he has to push and probe in the interview to learn everything he can about you. He has to stock up on ammunition because he has to sell you to the department head. He will, therefore, work to tear every positive fact he can out of you. Given a little push, most candidates will spill about themselves, but not nearly as much as a good recruiter will drag out of them.

The recruiter also has to probe for weaknesses. Sometimes he gets prosecutorial about it and jumps on the attack. He may get obnoxious and belligerent or ask personal questions. This tactic is frequently used in "stress interviews" (covered in chapter 7) to see how the candidate reacts to pressure. The recruiter has to uncover as many weaknesses as he can to make himself less vulnerable. If a department head, in a follow-up interview, discovers a glaring shortcoming in the candidate that the recruiter missed, the recruiter will have been caught napping.

The Recruiter as Salesperson...and Con Artist

The recruiter has to sell. Sometimes he has to sell a good candidate on the company or on the job. But it is after the recruiter has decided to recommend the candidate that the recruiter moves behind the scenes and goes into high sales gear. Rare is the recruiter who lets a candidate go "naked" into an interview with the department head. The recruiter goes into the big sell because:

• He frequently doesn't trust the department head's judgment.

• There is always a fair chance that without some advance billing the candidate would blow the interview.

Suppose a department manager asked the recruiter to find a good candidate for a secretarial job. If the recruiter settled on a good candidate, then called the department head and said, "Charlie, I've got a candidate for your secretary job," Charlie would, of course, ask, "What about her?" If the recruiter said, "Oh, she's okay," the department head wouldn't be very interested.

It's like a blind date. If a woman offering to fix a friend up with a man says, "He's not bad," that date probably will never happen. The fixer-upper has to get her friend's motor going. She has to tell her that he's an interesting guy, that he has something going for him. And that's the same routine the recruiter goes into.

First he picks his candidate. Then he gears up for the big sell.

Sometimes the big sell is the little con job. When the recruiter goes to see the department head to tout the candidate, the conversation might go something like this:

Recruiter: Charlie, you know that secretary's job you've been bugging me to fill?

Charlie: Do I know? Do I ever know! I'm going out of my mind with the backlog around here, and I'm losing another secretary next week.

Recruiter: Well, I've talked to 14 people this week trying to find you a secretary. (In reality he might have only talked to one. Numbers on a recruiting report can be about as accurate as many expense accounts — grossly inflated.) I've finally found you a good one. Belinda Lee.

Charlie: What's she like?

Recruiter: Very pleasant. Hell of a good typist. A little weak on shorthand, but...

Charlie: Oh, she's gotta be good on shorthand.

Recruiter: Charlie, I've never seen you dictate. Why don't you just babble into a tape recorder and she can transcribe. Ah, the hell with it, Charlie. There's an opening up in Purchasing where I think she'll fit better.

The recruiter turns around to start to leave, and Charlie invariably says, "Hold it! I've gotta talk to this girl. I'm short one secretary already, Angie's leaving Monday, everything's falling apart and..."

The recruiter comes back and says, "Oh, hell, I'd rather take her up to Purchasing. She's too good to work for you anyway...."

When the recruiter brings Belinda in to meet Charlie, *Charlie's ready*.

The recruiter works as much on the other end, priming department heads, as he does with the candidates. He has to, because he wants to keep his hiring average high. And that's the name of the game at every step of the way with you and the recruiter: the recruiter's hiring average.

Item B

The Roads to an Interview

The most important step in the hiring process is the interview. You must have it. There are four major roads to the interview:

• Answering Ads: You might have to push.

• The College Placement Center: All you have to do is sign up.

• Employment Agencies: An agent gets you your interview.

• Knocking on Doors: You might have to get tough.

The next four chapters examine those four avenues to the interview.

3

ADS

Discover what help-wanted ads really mean. Choose different answers for different kinds of ads

Very few people know how to read the help-wanted ads in the newspaper — that is, *really* read them.

You can read an ad, accept it at face value, conclude that you're not qualified for the job, and thereby pass up a good job you could have landed. If you understand what is behind a want ad, and if you read the ads properly, you won't make that mistake.

An ad usually is not the sign of a company making a little foray into the marketplace just to see who is out there. Nor is it a casual request for a new employee. It is a desperate scream for help emanating from somewhere deep in the corporate diaphragm, a sign that someone, somewhere, is in serious pain and needs a remedy.

Employers hate to place ads for several reasons:

• An ad releases competitive information into the marketplace. (The ABC Company is advertising for salespeople again. They must be having turnover problems.) (ABC is running an ad for a senior something. Their training program must be a flop.)

• An ad exposes employers to militants. The first phone call to come in after an ad has been placed is likely to be from a black organization asking if there are any blacks on this job now, or from a women's group wondering if women will be considered, or from a 63-year-old asking if age will disqualify him. The company might not be discriminating against anyone, but those questions make an employer squirm.

• An ad costs a lot of money. A two-column-by-four-inch ad in the Sunday edition of a big-city paper costs as much as a refrigerator-freezer. An ad the same size in the national edition of *The Wall Street Journal* costs as much as a trip to Europe for two. Those sums are not life and death to a large employer, but they aren't trifles, so management watches the results with interest, and the recruiter is judged by those results.

I once spent $1,400 of my company's money for a four-column-by-ten-inch newspaper ad that did not pull a single response. My boss came within a heartbeat of firing me, and I don't blame him. Something was wrong. I was the recruiter; I was supposed to know how to write an ad and when and where to place it. I was supposed to be close enough to the market to know that people were unavailable. "The next time you place $1,400 worth of advertising and get no action," my boss told me, "you don't work here any more."

Brutal? Perhaps. But that's the way it is, and recruiters accept being judged in this manner.

The point is that when you see an ad, there is a strong chance that you're looking at a recruiter who is in trouble and is being leaned on by higher management. The right people aren't coming in the front door, and he doesn't know where to turn up somebody for the job, so he turns to the want ad as a last resort. Then he prays.

When you answer an ad, you should be aware that the balance of power has shifted. The situation is much different than if you were making a cold call on an employer. You need a job; the recruiter has to fill a job. You need each other.

Overblown Ads

When the recruiter is forced to write an ad, he over-writes it tremendously. He never advertises for the minimum; he always tries to get the maximum he can ask for without looking silly. And because he has advertised for the maximum, *very, very often the recruiter does not expect the candidate he describes*. He may be less willing to give ground on some qualifications than on others, but he will almost always give ground.

The recruiter operates the same way as the home owner, the real estate agent, or the used car dealer. Take a look at your daily newspaper. You can probably find an ad in which some car dealer is asking $1,500 for a four-year-old Pontiac. He knows he will never get that price. Would you pay it? No, you would offer him $1,100 or so. Everybody knows $1,500 is just a starting price.

Let's turn now from used cars to "used" people.

Here's an example of a typical hiring decision. You decide, on the basis of this sketchy information, which candidate you would probably hire.

There was a newspaper ad a few years ago for a campus administrator. The ad said that the job required five years' experience and a master's degree. Here are the four finalists:

No. 1: A man with a national reputation. An outstanding individual, 63 years old, making about 140 percent of what you are prepared to pay. Plus you would have to pay him more than his present salary.

No. 2: Master's degree. Another outstanding candidate. But no experience. Twenty-two years old and right out of school.

No. 3: More than enough good experience, but only a bachelor's degree (and they pay a lot of attention to that "union card" on campus).

No. 4: Master's degree and seven years' experience. But under contract to another university. Not available for ten months. You would work a school year with an empty chair.

Which do you want: too much money? not enough experience? not enough education? not available? They hired number 3. Me.

You have to have a master's degree to hold my job of placement director at the University of Wisconsin – Milwaukee. It said so right in the ad. Yet I don't have one. And I don't think you could convince me that I need one to do my job properly.

It is true that for some jobs there are absolute requirements. If a firm is advertising for a corporate attorney, the candidate had better have a law degree. If a company wants a truck driver, any candidate who doesn't have a driver's license is going to be laughed out of the office. But a master's degree for my job? Nonsense.

When you read the newspaper ads, be careful to distinguish between absolute requirements and gee-we'd-like-to-haves. Remember that the ads are inflated, full of exaggeration and wishful thinking. You can be confident that the qualifications called for in an ad are overstated, and you should ignore them. If I had paid attention to the qualifications that were stated for the job I now hold, I wouldn't have applied for it.

Part of the reason recruiters set such high standards in ads is legal requirements. If a recruiter says in an ad that the qualifications for the job come to a total of 10 pounds of knowledge and experience, and if he hired someone with 14 pounds, everyone between 10 and 14 pounds has a valid unfair employment practices claim. So he doesn't advertise for 10; he lists 25 pounds, which is almost ridiculous. But when he hires at 14, nobody between 10 and 14 can complain — they didn't qualify either.

What many recruiters would really like to be able to say in an ad is: "Successful candidate will be able to change water into wine"; in other words, nobody will qualify.

What Can Happen to You?

When you answer an ad, only three things can happen to you. Two of them are good.

• Rejection. If you are turned down, you haven't lost much, because you didn't have the job when you went in. Try again somewhere else.

• Spin-off. The recruiter might tell you, "You don't fit the job I advertised in the paper, but I have another job in my desk drawer that wasn't listed. Want to talk about it?"

A high school junior in South Bend, Indiana, answered an ad for a busboy in a swanky restaurant. The restaurant manager liked the boy's style and appearance and told him, "We have another job we didn't mention in the ad that might appeal to you." He was hired as a doorman. He was issued a snappy uniform and put to work greeting customers and parking cars. He was paid 15 cents an hour more than the busboys, and he got lots of big tips, which busboys never got. The tips were especially high when the drunks rolled out at closing time (on Notre Dame football weekends it was like the Comstock Lode). Furthermore, he didn't have to grub around with dirty dishes, and he made a lot of good contacts around town.

The job you get in a spin-off will not always be a better job than the one advertised, but it can be a very good one.

> **TIP:** An ad that says "senior" (senior anything) should make your ears go up. A recruiter knows that if he has three jobs — senior, intermediate and junior — he will advertise only the senior

job. If he gets any kind of traffic at all, he will fill all three jobs.

• You can get the job.

If you do get the job, it will probably be the result of a compromise between the job specifications and your qualifications. Of the 8,000 people I hired, not one was the perfect candidate. There was something wrong with everybody. They were too young; their degree was a little bit off; they didn't have enough experience; they had too much experience; they cost too much — and on and on. Everyone is "kinda."

When the recruiter finds someone who satisfies him, he goes off in the corner with the supervisor and makes a deal. It goes like this: "Charlie, you know that Social Worker II job I'm trying to fill for you? I've had an ad in the State Employment Service listing for three weeks. I've talked to nothing but junk, and the paper that's coming across my desk is terrible. I'll tell you what. Kathy Burns is sitting in my office, and she's got it. Her head is screwed on real tight. She doesn't have a master's in social work, but she has a master's in counseling, and this is a counseling job. You want Kathy?"

Charlie says, "No. I want someone with a master's in social work. Now go out and find someone."

The recruiter says, "Okay, Charlie, let's talk about this for a minute. I'm not getting the kind of candidate you want. So I'm going to give you some options. We can go back to listing the ad with the State Employment Service, which is going to take another week in an already elongated hiring procedure; we can put an ad in the paper, and then I'm going to start charging you some money; we can cancel the opening (at this point, Charlie says, "You're crazy. I'm going under with too much work."); or you can talk to Kathy. Now what do you want to do?"

Charlie says, "You don't give me much choice." And he might hire Kathy.

Hiring is a science of retreat. The employer sets down what he wants in the new employee. Then he backs off from that position, then backs off some more, and then backs off a little more. Then he hires somebody.

Some Hints

Here are some more tips on how to read ads:

• When an ad says that the job pays "to $20,000," the employer will probably pay more. When the employer mentions $20,000, he's telling you what track he's on. He's telling anyone who is making $40,000 to forget it. And he's telling anyone who is making $10,000 that they probably won't make it.

• When the ad plugs the employer's locale with a phrase like "good hunting and fishing," the company is probably in a small town. That recruiter really does want somebody who likes hunting and fishing. An employer in Escanaba, Michigan, knows that if he hires an urbane person who is keenly interested in theater, the person probably won't be happy in the area and won't stay. But if he hires someone who enjoys tying into a muskie, he'll have a happy employee.

Recruiters sometimes will try to capitalize on the hobbies of candidates. A recruiter in Denver might watch the parking lot when an out-of-town applicant is coming for an interview. If there is a ski rack on the car, he might lower the monthly starting salary by 50 dollars.

A recruiter might question you in some depth about a hobby you listed on your resume. He might be trying to ascertain how much leverage he has over you — how willing you might be to take the job for less because it would give you good opportunities to pursue your hobby. Don't come off as a "super-buff." It could cost you money.

The recruiter might try other lines of questioning to learn your depth of interest in a community. He might ask you, "Have you ever been to Denver before?" If you say, "Yes. My wife and I vacationed here three years ago and we fell in love with it. We plan to retire here," you have given the recruiter a hammer that he can use on you.

• Some ads say "Equal Opportunity Employer," and some don't. If an ad does say that, it probably means that the organization is government related or has some federal contracts. Federal regulations require anyone doing business with the government to include that statement in help-wanted ads. That statement does not necessarily mean that the organization is determined to hire a minority group person for the job. The absence of that statement does not necessarily mean that the employer is not after minority group candidates.

• There there is the old "public relations" dodge. An ad will say you can make a lot of money in a good "public relations" job. Public relations is a specialized type of professional work. It involves writing, editing, and working with the news media. But some employers realize that many people don't know what public relations is, that many people feel public relations involves wining and dining people and other glamorous activities. When an ad says a job is in public relations, if it doesn't say something about writing or editing ability, the job probably is in sales. Although sales is an excellent and rewarding field, many people are turned off by it. So recruiters for sales jobs often resort to come-ons.

• The word "mature" in an ad shouldn't scare off anybody of any age. When an employer advertises for a "mature secretary," he probably has in mind someone over 40. But he might be impressed by a younger person with a strong sense of responsibility and good judgment.

I moonlight as a search consultant. In that role, I find managers and skilled technicians for companies. The name of my firm is David Neil & Associates. David is my older son's name; Neil is the younger boy. I use this fictitious name, as many recruiters do, so candidates don't call me at home. Often a recruiter will use two or three different names in ads in different newspapers so he can measure the activity each ad generates.

The following are some ads that I have written for corporate clients. (Addresses and phone numbers have been omitted.) They illustrate the overwriting I have described.

**We Seek An
EE or ME With
DIRTY BOOTS**

Our client has an immediate opening for a BSEE or BSME with 3 plus years in field testing. This LEAD ENGINEER will travel 30%-40% (rarely two consecutive weekends) to massive earth moving equipment operating in the field to devise testing setups, mount strain gauges and other measuring instruments, and gather the data required. This position can lead to a manager's spot and is the ideal assignment for the individual who seeks a challenge and variety of a "non-desk" job. Qualified candidates should call
DAVID NEIL
SEARCH CONSULTANTS

We would have gladly accepted an associate degree or someone who had good military electronics training plus one year of good experience. Maybe less.

SALESMAN

Our client has an immediate and attractive opening for a professional salesman. The successful candidate will have a college education and a proven background in sales to the capital goods industry. His strong points will include excellent ability in communication (both oral and written); be willing to travel 10%-25% of the time and be receptive to intensive training.

The plant is located in a rural community.

Only those who are aggressive, impressive and professional need call CE 0-0000 (collect calls accepted) or send resume including salary requirements to:
David Neil and Associates

Although the candidate selected had a college degree, several strong competing candidates did not. The college degree was pure overstatement. Two ads for the same job:

28

The individual hired did not have a degree, let alone a master's. He had strong Navy electronics. The M.S. is baloney.

The person selected for this top management job had a bachelor of science in mechanical engineering, no MBA, and a background as a successful sales manager. No marketing. No top management. And no knowledge of the electrical contracting market. Notice the "helpful but not required."

Some more examples of how to interpret qualifications called for in ads:

**PERSONNEL
ADMINISTRATOR**
We have an opening for a benefits administrator to handle pension plan administration, life health plan administration, etc. Will also be involved in salary administration and recruiting.
Degree required with a minimum of two years' personnel experience desired, preferably in benefits administration.

Plenty of soft spots in this ad. A degree is "required." Any degree. (And it probably *isn't* required.) A minimum of two years' experience is "desired," and that should "preferably" be in benefits administration.

They're wide open for any sharp, intelligent, competent candidate. Pay no attention to the "qualifications."

**DIRECTOR OF
SOCIAL SERVICES**
Hospital seeks a qualified individual to head its Social Services Department. The ideal candidate will have a MSW and administrative or supervisory experience.

They're looking for a "qualified individual." Well, you're certainly an individual, but are you qualified? Read on and find out what that means.

It says the "ideal candidate" will have a master's in social work and some experience at bossing.

Not true. The "ideal candidate" will be the one who impresses them the most. Don't worry about the master's degree.

30

If your background is in social work or any related field, you have a good shot at the job.

SALES REP
We have an immediate opening for an individual with a minimum of five years' experience selling paper products.
Your work history should indicate your ability to produce results with a minimum of supervision.

Pay no attention to that stuff about five years' experience. If you want to sell paper and can "indicate your ability to produce results," apply for the job.

SALES MANAGEMENT & ADMINISTRATION
Rapidly growing manufacturer has an opening in the sales and marketing department.
Company seeks an individual whose goals are geared to a career in management.

Many people will read the heavy type and go on to the next ad. Read this ad. They are looking for someone who someday would like to manage — that's you!

Don't let heavy headlines scare you away from ad content.

CORPORATE BUYER
Fortune 500 subsidiary seeks a corporate buyer who will be responsible for purchasing tools and other miscellaneous items. Should have at least two years' industrial buying experience with college degree preferred.

"*Should have* at least two years industrial buying experience."

"College degree *preferred*."

"Should have" and "preferred" are cop-out words. They indicate "gee-we'd-like-to-have." They're meaningless.

What this ad really means is that you don't have to have two years' experience or a degree. They want somebody who can do the job. That's all.

Answering the Ad

Many job applicants think their resume will land them the job. It won't. If a newspaper ad tells you to send a resume, don't do it (unless you have no choice, such as answering an ad for a job in Tucson when you live in New York.) Don't phone, either.

If you sent a resume, you simply are giving the recruiter a tool to turn you down. You may have outstanding qualifications for the job, but you could lose out because of a quirk — maybe you have an Italian name and the recruiter doesn't like Italians (a cynical statement, but not a far-fetched situation, since recruiters are not free of prejudice).

If the recruiter reads your resume and decides to turn you down, he marks *R&F* (regret and file) in the corner of your resume and slips it into the out basket. He has spent maybe 15 seconds on you. If you phone, he will force you into a little interview on the phone. Again, you would be giving him the tools to reject you: he is not going to hire you over the phone, but he might reject you.

If you want that job, go in the front door.

You can spend the rest of your life sending resumes. You are not going to get that job unless you sit down with the decision maker and communicate your interest in the job with attitude, with facial expression, with body English and so forth. There is no way you can put your excitement on paper.

The yarn I tell students about how I got my job illustrates the importance of going in for an interview rather than sending a resume.

he ad in the paper said the university wanted a placement director. It said the person must have five years of related experience plus a master's degree. It went on to say that candidates should send their resume to the dean. (This was the first request for a resume.)

I had the experience, but not the master's. I realized that most of the other candidates would have master's degrees. If I had sent my resume to the dean, he probably would have read it and been turned off by my lack of an advanced degree. I figured I could get him to give ground on the master's degree, but I knew I would have to talk to him in person to do it. Had I sent my resume in, it probably would have been thrown out. So I ignored the request for the resume.

The next day I called the dean's office and asked for him. The receptionist said, "May I tell him who's calling?" Then I hung up. All I wanted to know was whether he was in or not, and her question told me he was.

I hustled over to the dean's office and told the receptionist that I wanted to talk to the dean about the placement job. In the 10 minutes it had taken me to get to the dean's office, he had slipped out. The receptionist said he probably would be gone for quite awhile and added, "If you'd like, I can take your resume and give it to him when he returns." (This was the second request for a resume.) I said, "No, that's okay. I'll wait."

About 15 minutes later, a man about 40 years old walked past me, went into the dean's office, and shut the door. The dean, obviously.

A few seconds later, the receptionist's phone buzzed, she answered it and began whispering into the phone. I started to laugh, and she started to get red. I could imagine the conversation:

Dean: Who's *that?*

Receptionist: I don't know. He wants to see you about the placement job.

Dean: Well, I'm too busy now.

But he was trapped, and he knew it. About 10 minutes later, the dean opened the door and began wheeling out of the office. By the time he had gotten four steps into the room, I was standing in front of him with my hand sticking out for him to shake. "Dean, my name is Kirby Stanat, and I'd like to take a few minutes of your time to talk about the placement job."

Not having much choice, he shook my hand. Then he said he was "awfully busy this morning" and asked me if I could leave my resume with the receptionist so he could look it over some time in the next couple of days (third request for a resume). I said, "Well, I would like to talk to you briefly, some time at your convenience. I do have some questions." How could he refuse? The request was reasonable: a few minutes at his convenience. If he had said, "Make an appointment," I would have made the appointment and stuck the resume back in my pocket, because if I left my resume, he would have been going over it before I got to the parking lot. As it happened, he said, "Why don't we talk now. Come into my office."

Bingo. Interview! We talked for an hour; then I left.

What happened next? In the next few days, the dean got a batch of resumes in the mail. On his desk were two stacks. In one stack were the resumes of the 30 people he hadn't met; in the other stack was the resume of Stanat, who he had met. *I now became the minimum standard against which everybody else was measured.* It wouldn't make sense to talk to somebody who had lesser qualifications than mine.

The dean dipped into the pile of resumes. He looked over the first one and decided, "Hmm, not as good as Stanat." Out.

He picked up number two. "Definitely not as good as Stanat, even though this candidate has a master's degree. Stanat's experience looks better." Out.

Number three. "Yeh, this one looks as good as Stanat. Maybe better." And he put it over in the other pile.

But the point is that *I started that pile.* Instead of competing against 30 people, I competed against only a handful.

The larger point of the story is that if I had done what the ad told me—if I had obediently sent a resume or if I had followed anybody's instructions along the line—I wouldn't have landed the job.

Don't wait for an invitation. Go directly to the decision maker. If you live in Little Rock and read an ad for a job you want in Dallas, you should go to Dallas. If you don't have a car, fly, take a bus, hitchhike. And get there as soon as you can. Don't wait a week; otherwise the edge you would have had by being first will be lost. Being first is important. Many employers grab the first qualified person who comes along, and later applicants are told, "I'm sorry, but that job has been filled."

When you look through the want-ad section of a newspaper, read the ads—really *read* them closely. There may be less there—and more for you—than there first appears to be. The sample want-ads included later in this chapter show how newspaper ads should be read and followed up.

REGIONAL SALES MANAGER
A well-established clothing manufacturer offers an excellent opportunity and bright future for an aggressive, sales-minded person with experience.
Position entails some travel. Car necessary; all expenses paid. Write fully in confidence: Joe Jones, Clothing, Inc., 111 Main Street, Los Angeles, California.

Look at that! If the job is of interest to you, go see Joe. You know his name and his address, and it would be simple to get his phone number, if necessary.

Apply directly in person, with no prior contact.

MANAGERS FOR FAST FOOD RESTAURANTS
We need three persons with restaurant managerial experience to operate three of our restaurants in the metropolitan area.
The individuals hired will have complete charge of the restaurants: hiring, training and supervising employees, as well as increasing trade and managing finances.
If you are looking for a career with advancement opportunity, we want to talk with you.
Call 111-1111
Quick-Chow Restaurants

Notice that the ad gives you the name of the outfit and the phone number. If you look up Quick-Chow in the phone book, you might find a listing for their local headquarters. Cross-check the phone number with the numbers of all the Quick-Chow restaurants in town. If one of the restaurants has the phone number that's given in the ad, that's probably where you should go—without phoning! That little bit of research to get the address and your subsequent personal visit might make the difference.

The Blind Ad

An ad that asks you to apply in writing to a newspaper box or post office box and does not list the employer's name is a blind ad. The blind ad is a screen behind which a company can do all sorts of things it can't do when it identifies itself in an ad.

When a company identifies itself, every person who answers the ad must be treated in a professional way. A file is set up for each applicant, and every applicant gets at least a return letter. The processing cost can be 10 to 15 dollars per applicant. If an ad draws a hundred responses, the company is spending a lot of money on people it is not going to hire. But when you send your resume to Anonymous, Inc., at a post office box, the company can pitch out your resume without spending a nickel on you.

There are many reasons why companies run blind ads. They don't want their competition to know what they're up to; they don't want their employees to know what they're up to; they don't want their customers to know what they're up to. But perhaps the main reason for running a blind ad these days is that they don't want *you*, the job seeker, to know what they're up to. A blind ad makes it easy for a company to discriminate—against women, blacks, whites, anybody over 40, Ivy League graduates—anybody.

In some states, the only way you can find out who placed a blind ad is to get a law enforcement agency, such as the district attorney's office or the state attorney general's office, to subpoena an executive of the newspaper and ask the newspaper, in court, who placed the ad. To get a DA or attorney general to serve a subpoena, you have to convince him that there is some evidence of discrimination. That is hard to do when you don't know the name of the employer or the employer's intent. So it's a tight circle, with the employer safe inside.

Since the blind ad gives the employer so many advantages, why don't all companies run all of their help-wanted ads blind? Because they don't pull as well. On several occasions as a recruiter, I have placed two ads in the same paper for the same job with almost the same wording. One ad listed the company by name, the other was blind. In every case, the blind ad pulled about 40 percent of the response the other ad pulled.

Many people consider blind ads an insult. They figure, "If I answer this ad, they're going to know who I am, but I won't know who they are. The hell with them."

So how do you respond to a blind ad? If you want the job, there is not much you can do beyond playing their game and sending your resume in.

Unless...you want to do some detective work. Sometimes you can figure out who is placing the blind ad. One company has run blind ads saying, "Major machine tool manufacturer located on Highway AA has opening for...." There is only one major machine tool manufacturer on Highway AA.

Job-Wanted Ads

Do recruiters pore over the ads job seekers place in newspapers and trade publications? There must be some employers who read those ads. But I don't know any.

Nevertheless, it might be worth a few dollars to advertise yourself. If you do, your chances will probably be better if your ad is serious in tone rather than "cute."

Most executives would respond better to an ad that says:

Assistant sales manager with high-quality, medium-sized company seeks sales manager's job with medium-sized or large organization. Outstanding record in sales and management (6 yrs. sales, 3 yrs. management). Strong references.

---

than they would to one that says:

Hey, Mister Corporation President:
Wanna move your sales force off
dead center? Want a man who can
motivate 'em with just the right
amount of encouragement and good
old-fashioned whip-cracking? Sign
me on as your sales manager, then
sit back, light up a $2 cigar, and
watch my smoke.

The first guy comes off as a professional, the second as
a jerk.

Item C

Where to Apply

In almost every instance, apply to the personnel department or employment office. That's the headquarters
for all hiring. It is the keeper of employment requisitions
and applications. It is, therefore, the only place in the
organization that knows of openings all over the organization and is the only department that will give your
application some flexibility — that is, make you available
to more than one department or function. In addition, this
is the department most likely to cave in to some of the
tactics described elsewhere in this book.

If you send your application to the president, his secretary will probably open it, see that it is a resume, and
route it to the personnel department for handling. Personnel people are often annoyed by these applications and
resumes and treat them more harshly than those sent
directly to their department.

There are few exceptions when you should apply somewhere other than personnel. One is when you really know
someone in authority in the organization. Another is
when you are a high-level executive.

THE PLACEMENT CENTER

Use it to your advantage

The college placement center is like an auto showroom where recruiters are constantly shopping for sporty new models. The recruiters *want* to talk to students, and they have jobs, jobs they must fill. If you're in your last year of college and if you want a job after you graduate, the placement center is a must for you. It's your best shot.

Consider facts such as these:

• IBM hired 80 to 85 percent of its professional people through college recruiting.

• In 1975, almost every employer who sent a recruiter to Vassar hired at least one graduating student. The placement director said some banks hired as many as five people.

• Also in 1975, an extremely grim year for job seekers, students who interviewed through the Placement Office for the Graduate School of Business of the University of Chicago averaged about 20 interviews apiece. They got an average of two and one-half job offers each. Not bad. In more prosperous years the average was three and one-half offers.

Placement directors all over the country can provide similar statistics to demonstrate the advantage of working through the college placement center.

The placement center eliminates one major hurdle in the job-hunting process — getting an interview. You don't have to get past an officious receptionist; you don't have to go up against a busy personnel officer who may not want to talk to you. All you have to do is sign up at the placement center with the recruiters whose companies you're interested in.

The placement center is also the perfect place to sharpen your interviewing skills. If you start taking interviews early in your last year of school, you should be an astute interviewee by the second semester.

Placement people at universities all over the country constantly lament the fact that too many students ignore their services. You should get to know the placement director on your campus. Nobody else is plugged in to as many entry level jobs in your area as the placement director. Some time early in your last year of school, or even the year before, make an appointment to meet the placement director.

Treat that interview as if it were an interview with a recruiter. Dress up. Take a resume with you and act like a professional. That will impress the placement director. Impressing him is important — maybe he knows about some good jobs that he can steer you to.

When you start interviewing with recruiters, check in with the placement director occasionally to discuss your interviews. If your placement director is good, he or she can give you valuable advice about how you are handling yourself.

Sometimes a company personnel officer or a department head will call me at my university placement office and put in a panicky request for a couple of candidates for a job. "Today's Monday," the corporate official will say. "We need somebody on the payroll by Thursday. We don't want 600 candidates down here tying everything up, and we can't go through your silly procedures. So please don't post the job. Instead, would you give me a couple of names?" Often I'll give them a couple of names or tell some students about the job.

My obligation is to every student who is graduating from my university, and ideally every student should have an equal shot at every job. So the question of whether a placement director should do any prescreening of candidates for an employer is open to debate. But in a situation where an employer is genuinely desperate, I must provide a few names. If I don't, that employer will go to someone at another university who will. If I suspect that the employer is not really desperate and is just trying to get around the standard procedure, I won't do it.

There is another reason for getting to know your placement director. He can give recruiters insights about you that they might otherwise miss. The placement director might tell a recruiter, "Initially, you're not going to like this guy; he's done poorly in interviews. But he's an excellent candidate. He has an extremely analytical mind, and he's loaded with integrity. He just doesn't come off well in the first interview."

So if you're smart, you'll get to know the placement director well enough that he or she knows you by your first name.

How Placement Centers Work

Placement centers are operated and paid for by the college or university as a service to students. They vary in scope and operation. There are basically three systems for deciding which students will interview with which employers.

• The Open Sign-Up System. If a company recruiter is scheduled for 30 interviews, the first 30 students who sign up get interviews. (Sometimes obviously unqualified students are removed from the list — for example, a political science graduate signing up with a recruiter who wants to talk only to electrical engineering graduates.)

• The Staff Sign-Up System. A counselor in the placement center helps students sign up with the right employers.

• The Card System. Each graduating student gets a batch of top-priority cards plus lower-priority cards. Students submit cards for the companies they want to interview with. If a student is anxious to interview with a particular company, he turns in a high-priority card. If he is lukewarm about the company, he can submit a lesser-priority card. Students who submit high-priority cards get first crack at interviewing. If the company has interview time left over, lower-priority cards are honored.

There are variations. The Placement Office for the University of Chicago's Graduate School of Business uses a bidding system that was developed by the students. Each student starts the fall quarter with 200 points and the winter quarter with 350 points. The students then bid on the companies whose recruiters they want to interview with. A bid of 50 or 60 points is usually enough to get an interview. The office also has each student work up a resume in September. The resumes are made into a resume book and sent to employers who regularly call at the school. Richard Thain, placement director, said:

> Part of the basis of this system is that this school allows the company to have one invitational schedule as long as the company will mount on the bulletin board one open schedule. This enables the companies to make use of the resume book. This is all part of our belief here that the companies should do some prescreening, if possible. We want them to work at it. The company ought to do its homework, if it's serious, and identify some of the people they want to see. Just about everybody here gets some invitations.

If a company invites a student to interview, the student spends only two points.

Thain said the school departed from "the long line system" in the late 1960s. "We decided that one should not treat students like cattle, waiting in long lines." First the school tried a lottery system with students drawing straws for some of the popular companies. (Some schools still use lotteries.) Then, in 1973, the bidding system was adopted.

At most big universities, the placement center is a large facility. Some placement centers offer career counseling, some conduct workshops on getting a job, and most maintain a well-stocked library of information about employers. The professional schools and specialized undergraduate schools, such as journalism, business, or education, at many big universities maintain separate placement offices operated either by a full-time placement specialist or a faculty member. (The all-university placement center deals in jobs in those areas, too, so you should check in at both your departmental placement office and the all-university center.)

Whatever the placement system on your campus is, you should learn how it works and use it. If you pass up the bonanza of employee-seeking recruiters who come to your campus, what's left for you is answering help-wanted ads and making cold calls. And that's a tough league.

> **TIP:** If you go to a small private college that is not on the recruiting circuit for most companies, and if there is a big state school nearby, see if you can use the placement center at the university.

Why Do They Bother with Green Graduates?

The typical recruiter's college swing through the Midwest includes Ohio State, Purdue, Illinois – Chicago Circle, Minnesota, and several other campuses. He may interview from 70 to 100 people for four or five jobs. Why is he doing this at all? Why is his company spending money to send him around to talk to a bunch of green

44

college seniors? No mystery — to save money. College seniors become "entry level personnel," and entry level people come cheap. They're a real bargain for the employer. When a department head submits his budget, he budgets several hundred dollars for each new college graduate he expects to hire. That is what it costs the company to hire you, including all recruiting costs: the recruiter's travel, advertising, brochures, and a return visit by the candidate to the corporate headquarters or the plant.

On the next rung up — for instance two years' experience — the price goes up. The company probably has to do newspaper advertising at this level. It may have to relocate the experienced person and his or her family, their two-year-old set of living room furniture, and their new bedroom set. The cost of hiring somebody like that is a lot more than a few hundred dollars.

At the executive level, it can cost the company $20,000 or more to hire the right person. That's before the new executive ever sets foot in the office or knows the way to the washroom.

Finding middle and top management people usually includes expensive and widely circulated newspaper ads, extensive recruiter and candidate travel, and perhaps the cost of retaining an executive search firm. If the chosen candidate is already an executive, the cost of relocating his family and belongings zooms. He is accustomed to "the perks" (executive perquisites — goodies) and is not at all shy about asking for them. It is not unusual for an executive to demand that his new employer pay the real estate fee for selling his present house. He may also demand that the new company give him an allowance to paint, drape, and carpet his new house. Then the company might discover that the new executive is a rock hound and wants the company to pay for moving the seven tons of rocks in his basement; or that he owns blue ribbon horses or cattle that have to be hauled to a new pasture; or that his gigantic boat, now floating in Tampa Bay, must do its future floating in Puget Sound. That may seem to you like the executive is long on gall, but the company frequently agrees, because it needs the talents of this tiger shark.

Obviously the company does well to recruit entry level people at a few hundred dollars apiece. The company knows that within a few years some of the people it hired at entry level will jump to other companies, but it also knows that some of those entry level people will rise to management in the company and will save the company the cost of looking elsewhere for new executives. What all of this means is that if you're a college student, companies need you.

But Why You?

Companies need you. Or, rather, a company needs perhaps 10 entry level people. And 300 are interested in working for that company. That gets to the heart of your problem. And the recruiter's problem. How are you going to convince the recruiter that you're what he needs? What does he have going for him to help him decide which 10 of the 300 students are the right 10?

What the campus recruiter has to work with is some data and his own intuition. That is not much. And that is what college recruiters feel is the dark side of the job — that they have to make professionally binding decisions on evidence that is dangerously thin.

Look at the information they have to go on. Almost every student the recruiter talks to is going to get a degree. The degree, therefore, is a common denominator, and any statistician knows that a common denominator is not a good selector.

The most obvious variable statistic for a college student is grade point average. Some employers consider grade point a good indicator of ability to do well on a job, but others consider it m aningless. There are other hard facts, such as age, marital status, extracurricular activities, summer and part-time work, but the differences among candidates in those areas are usually insignificant. The result is that the recruiter is going to recommend the candidate he likes best. It's that simple: the one he *likes* best.

To illustrate that point, let's take two candidates from the same school. The recruiter must decide between them. They have very clear ideas of who they are. They know themselves, their strong points, their weaknesses, their peculiarities, their innermost selves. If they were introduced to each other, they naturally would feel that they were very different people. But here is how they appear on the data sheets the recruiter is going to take home with him:

Candidate A	**Candidate B**
Name: Jack Smith	Name: Marjorie Brown
Major: History	Major: History
Geographical Restrictions: None	Geographical Restrictions: None
Grade point: 2.9	Grade point: 3.1
Marital Status: Single	Marital Status: Single
Age: 23	Age: 22
Previous Work: Delivery truck driver, shoe store clerk	Previous Work: Bartender at college bar, camp counselor

What does the recruiter see? Not much. The two candidates have a two-tenths of a point difference in grade point. Will he base his standing back at the home office on that two-tenths? Certainly not. He is going to decide which one impressed him more in the interview, based on all the minor details of appearance, manners, general bearing, speech, and awareness of the work. The one who came across better. In other words, the one he liked.

Not As a "Student"

To succeed in campus job interviews, you have to know where that recruiter is coming from. The simple answer is that he is coming from corporate headquarters.

That may sound obvious, but it is a significant point that too many students do not consider. The recruiter is not a free spirit as he flies from Berkeley to New Haven, from Chapel Hill to Boulder. He's on an invisible leash to the office, and if he is worth his salary, he is mentally in corporate headquarters all the time he's on the road. If you can fix that in your mind — that when you walk into that bare-walled eight-by-ten cubicle in the placement center you are walking into a branch office of Sears, Bendix, or General Motors — you can avoid a lot of little mistakes and maybe some big ones. If, for example, you assume that because the interview is on campus the recruiter expects you to look and act like a student, you're in for a shock. A student is somebody who drinks beer, wears blue jeans, and throws a Frisbee. No recruiter has jobs for student Frisbee whizzes.

A cool spring day in late March. Sam Davis, a good recruiter who has been on the college circuit for years, is on my campus talking to candidates. He comes out to the waiting area to meet the student who signed up for an 11 o'clock interview. I'm standing in the doorway of my office, taking in the scene.

Sam calls the candidate: "Sidney Student." There sits Sidney. He's at a 45-degree angle, his feet are in the aisle, and he's almost lying down. He's wearing well-polished brown shoes, a tasteful pair of brown pants, a light brown shirt, and a good-looking tie. Unfortunately, he tops off this well-coordinated outfit with his Joe's Tavern Class A Softball Championship jacket, which has a big woven emblem over the heart. If that isn't bad enough, in his left hand is a cigarette and in his right hand is a half-eaten apple.

When Sam calls his name, the kid is caught off guard. He ditches the cigarette in an ashtray, struggles to his feet, and transfers the apple from the right to the left hand. Apple juice is everywhere, so Sid wipes his hand on the seat of his pants and shakes hands with Sam. Sam, who by now is close to having a stroke, gives me that what-the-hell-do-I-have-here look and has the young man follow him into the interviewing room.

The situation deteriorates even further — into pure Laurel and Hardy. The kid is stuck with the half-eaten apple, doesn't know what to do with it, and obviously is suffering some discomfort. He carries the apple into the interviewing room with him and places it in the ashtray on the desk — right on top of Sam's freshly lit cigarette. The interview lasts five minutes.

I have told that story to scores of students and have asked them, "Did that kid get the job?" Invariably, they answer, "No, he didn't," and, of course, they're right. The students readily accept the idea that the kid lost the job in the waiting room. No student has ever asked me, "Did Sam Davis investigate to find out if the kid had any talent?" or "Did Sam Davis ask around to see if the kid might be smarter than that?" Of course, Sam did not.

After Sam gave Sidney the lightning brush-off, I asked Sidney to come into my office. I slammed the door and started to chew him out, because a stunt like that reflects badly on the university and on the placement center, and, most important, it certainly doesn't do Sidney any good. I told him, "You handled yourself like some dumb student," and he said, "Well, Mr. Stanat, that's what I am. I am a student." I had to do a lot of talking to convince him that he had blown the interview, that Sam Davis wanted a professional, not a student.

That was an extreme case, but similar things happen, in varying degrees, over and over again in campus placement offices all over the country.

Recruiters want to meet professionals — with professional attitudes, professional objectives, and professional clothes. Behave and dress for the campus interview as if you were going to talk to the president of Ford Motor Company in his office.

The Inspection

Let us move in for a closer look at how the campus recruiter operates.

Let's say you have a 10 o'clock appointment with the recruiter from XYZ Corporation. The recruiter gets rid of the candidate in front of you at about 5 minutes to 10, jots down a few notes about what he is going to do with him or her, then picks up your resume or data sheet. (Students usually fill out standard data sheets provided by the placement center. Sometimes they give the placement center copies of their resumes. These are given to the recruiter before the interview. Later chapters of this book will strongly advise you, in certain situations, not to submit your resume before meeting the recruiter. That does not apply when you go through the college placement center. The reason for not submitting your resume in advance in some other situations is that submitting it could prevent you from getting an interview. But at the placement center, once you sign up for the interview, your interview is guaranteed.)

The importance of your data sheet or resume comes into play here. Although the recruiter is still in the interview room and you are still in the lobby, your interview is under way. You're on. The recruiter will look over your sheet pretty carefully before he goes out to call you. He develops a mental picture of you. He thinks, "I'm going to enjoy talking with this kid," or, "This one's going to be a turkey." The recruiter has already begun to make a screening decision about you.

His first impression of you, from reading the sheet, could come from your grade point. It could come from misspelled words. It could come from poor erasures or from the fact that necessary information is missing. By the time the recruiter has finished reading your sheet, you've already hit the plus or minus column. You might not be very far into either column, but you probably didn't land squarely on the neutral line dividing the two columns. I defy anybody to read 10 data sheets or resumes without forming an opinion about all 10 candidates.

Let's assume the recruiter got a fairly good impression from your sheet.

Now the recruiter goes out to the lobby to meet you. He almost shuffles along, and his mind is somewhere else. Then he calls your name, and at that instant he visibly clicks into gear. He just went to work. As he calls your name, he looks quickly around the room, waiting for somebody to move. If you are sitting on the middle of your back, with a book open and a cigarette going, and if you have to rebuild yourself to stand up, the interest will run right out of the recruiter's face. You, not the recruiter, made the appointment for 10 o'clock, and the recruiter expects to see a young professional come popping out of that chair like today is a good day and you're anxious to meet him.

At this point, the recruiter does something rude. He doesn't walk across the room to meet you halfway. He waits for you to come to him. Something very important is happening. He wants to see you move. He wants to get an impression about your posture, your stride, and your briskness. If you slouch over to him, sidewinderlike, he is not going to be impressed. He'll figure you would probably slouch your way through workdays. He wants you to come at him with lots of good things going for you. If you watch the recruiter's eyes, you can see the inspection. He glances quickly at shoes, pants, coat, shirt; dress, blouse, hose — the whole works.

He'll stick out his hand and say, "Good morning, Bill, my name is Joe Recruiter." Your handshake is extremely important.

> **TIP:** I would rather have a man bring me to my knees with a powerful handshake than give me a weak one. I suggest to women that they should not offer their hand to a male recruiter who doesn't stick his hand out first. There are still some sexists around, and many older recruiters react negatively to a woman walking up and sticking out a "paw."

Next the recruiter will probably say, "Okay, Bill, please follow me," and he'll lead you into his interviewing room.

When you get to the room, you may find that the recruiter will open the door and gesture you in — with him blocking part of the doorway. There's enough room for you to get past him, but it's a near thing.

As you scrape past, he gives you a closeup inspection. He looks at your hair; if it's greasy, that will bother him. He looks at your collar; if it's dirty, that will bother him. He looks at your shoulders; if they're covered with dandruff, that will bother him. If you're a man, he looks at your chin. If you didn't get a close shave, that will irritate him. If you're a woman, he checks your makeup. If it's too heavy, he won't like it.

Then he smells you. An amazing number of people smell bad. Occasionally a recruiter meets a student who smells like a canal horse. That student can expect an interview of about 4 or 5 minutes (the average interview is 25 to 30 minutes). Students who stretch their budgets don't have their clothes dry-cleaned often enough. And every recruiting season a recruiter will run into somebody who stopped at a student union before the interview to wolf down a hamburger with onions and a beer, then tried to cover up the smell with breath mints. That doesn't work. The kid ends up smelling like onions, beer, and breath mints, and the interview has been severely damaged.

Next the recruiter inspects the back side of you. He checks your hair (is it combed in front but not in back?), your heels (are they run down?), your pants (are they baggy?), your slip (is it showing?), your stockings (do they have runs in them?).

Then he invites you to sit down.

At this point, I submit, *the recruiter's decision on you is 75 to 80 percent made.*

Think about it. The recruiter has read your resume. He knows who you are and where you are from. He knows your marital status, your major, and your grade point. And he knows what you've done with your summers. He has inspected you, exchanged greetings with you, and smelled you. There is very little additional hard information that he must gather on you. From now on, it's mostly body chemistry.

Many recruiters have argued strenuously that they don't make such hasty decisions. So I tried an experiment. I told several recruiters that I would hang around in the hall outside the interview room when they took candidates in.

I told them that as soon as they had definitely decided not to recommend the candidate they were interviewing, they should snap their fingers loud enough for me to hear. It went like this:

First candidate: 38 seconds after the candidate sat down: Snap! Second candidate: 1 minute, 42 seconds: Snap! Third candidate: 45 seconds: Snap!

One recruiter was particularly adamant. "Hell, no," he said; he didn't rush to judgment on candidates. I asked him to participate in the snapping experiment. He went out in the lobby, picked up his first candidate of the day, and headed for an interview room. As he passed me in the hall, he glared at me. And his fingers went "Snap!"

What happens between you and the recruiter in these first few minutes is similar to the decisions that are made every night in singles bars. A young man sitting at the bar sees a woman walk in. He checks her out as best he can in the smoky, dimly lit atmosphere and decides whether he will venture forth. (It could, of course, be the other way around, the woman deciding whether or not she will make a move.) In about three minutes, he is standing beside her saying "Hi." She looks at him, checks him out. And she's not checking his ability to quote Shakespeare, or program computers, or for anything but the most superficial qualities. She decides whether or not she finds him attractive. If she does, she might talk to him. If not, she might turn away and ignore him. Meanwhile, he's deciding, too. When she turns to look at him, he does the same kind of inventory on her that she did on him, and he decides whether he's up off his stool to get change for cigarettes or to launch the big program.

Both of these people involved in the barroom hustle have made an essentially nonverbal decision. They have decided, "Forget it. A loser," or they have decided, "I think I want to go a little farther with this relationship."

That is the kind of decision the recruiter makes. If you have impressed him up to the point where you sit down

54

for the heart of the interview, he will want to get to know you better. From that point on, it is very easy to destroy a good impression, but almost impossible for you to turn a bad first impression around.

What Happens after the Interview?

When you walk out of the interview room,* you don't know whether you have a chance at the job or not.

If you failed, you'll know soon. Within a week or 10 days, you will get a letter telling you that you didn't make it. If you succeeded, it might be several weeks before you find out that they want you to come in for a second interview.

When your interview is over, ask the recruiter, "When should I expect to hear from you?" If he says two weeks, wait two weeks plus two days. Then call his office. (In the interview, you should ask where the recruiter is headquartered or where else you can get in touch with him.)

Strange things happen to resumes and files on applicants when they start traveling around the company bureaucracy. The recruiter might take your file back to company headquarters and send it up to Charlie, a department head. Three or four days later, the recruiter might call Charlie and ask him, "Did you get that file I sent you?" and Charlie might say, "Yeah, but he didn't seem to fit for my department, so I shipped it over to Al." And maybe Al never got it. Or threw it out. Or misplaced it.

Don't be surprised if you call to find out what they have decided to do about you and the recruiter or his secretary says, "I'm sorry, we can't put our hands on your application right now. Will you send us another resume?" It happens all the time.

Other weird things can happen. The airline can lose the recruiter's briefcase. Or in that two-week or two-month

*The interview is covered in Chapters 7 to 12.

waiting period, the recruiter can change jobs or be fired, and the company may decide to scrap all of his fieldwork.

Some companies like to play games. Their recruiter will tell several candidates, "We'll be in touch with you by May 15" and not contact anybody. They just wait for the phone to ring. They figure that the people who are really interested in working for them will contact them. They figure that the candidates who don't phone aren't aggressive enough to work for them.

> **CAUTION:** Do not be lulled into a false sense of success just because the recruiter is cordial to you and *seems* to be impressed by you. Some students come out of a pleasant interview with a recruiter and think they have the job locked up. With this confidence, they stop looking — until they get jerked back to reality when they pull a letter out of the mail that says, "Sorry, but right now we...." Recruiters are public relations emissaries of their organizations. In most cases, they are not going to deliberately alienate you. Some companies tell their recruiters, "Remember that any candidate you talk to might some day be a purchasing agent for a company that we want to sell something to."

Alumni Can Get Help, Too

> If you are several years out of college and are looking for a job, don't forget about the placement center at your alma mater. Placement centers deal mostly with entry level jobs, but the placement director is in touch with the market and frequently hears of a good job for an experienced person. Some universities offer special alumni placement services.
>
> At the college placement center, graduates can also get counseling about finding a job. The

people at the placement center can help you with your resume and with interview techniques.

Barbara A. Kopplin, a placement official at Marquette University, said:

We give some of our alumni an awful lot of counseling and attention. We have some alumni that I have spent 40 or 50 hours apiece on. One person who has been out of work for a year had worked himself up to a very high level in his field. In his quest to get even higher, he made a few fast job changes, and some of them were not an improvement. He didn't know when to quit — and when not to quit. His employment history doesn't look very good. He's a very capable person, but he has a lousy-looking resume.

That's the sort of problem a college placement center can help you solve.

University placement centers have a reciprocal arrangement, so you can use placement centers at colleges other than the one you graduated from.

Placement centers can help. And they're free.

Item D

Code

The College Placement Council, Inc., has adopted these guidelines for students, employers, and placement center personnel.

Employers

In direct on-campus recruiting activities, an employing organization is best represented by

its own personnel. In all other recruiting activities, the employing organization is expected to
assume responsibility for all representations
made in its name and in accordance with the
*Principles and Practices of College Career Plan-
ning, Placement, and Recruitment.*

The presentation of career job information should be
made in a knowledgeable, ethical, and responsible fash-
ion.

Ethical salary administration principles are expected
to be followed.

Special payments, gifts, bonuses, or other inducements
should not be offered.

All conditions of employment, including starting
salaries, should be explained clearly to candidates prior to
or at the time of the offer of employment.

Reasonable time to consider an offer should be given
candidates. In no case should candidates be subjected to
undue pressure to make a decision concerning employment.

An employment offer is made in good faith with sincere
intention to honor the commitment.

Preferential service should not be requested of any college placement office.

Individual salary offers made by other employers
should not be solicited by an employer.

Career Planning and Placement Personnel

The candidate's freedom of choice in the selection of a
career or a position should be protected from undue influence by faculty and placement staff.

Pertinent information should be made available to employers by the placement office.

Salary offers made by an individual employer should
not be divulged to other employers.

58

Referral of an employed graduate must be preceded by that person's request for active status.

Preferential service should not be extended to employers or candidates.

Communication and exchange of information between employers, students, faculty members, and administrators should be fostered. However, an employer should not be required to present and defend a corporate position before college and university groups as a condition for recruiting on campus.

Candidates

Both written and oral material presented by a candidate should be an honest statement of relevant data.

Reimbursement for visits at an employer's expense should be only for those expenditures pertinent to the trip. If other employers are visited on the same trip, the cost should be prorated.

The employer's deadline for acceptance of offers of employment should be met unless an extension has been obtained from the employer.

If candidates have legitimate reasons for the extended consideration of more than one offer, they should not only notify employers whose offers they are refusing, but also communicate with employers under consideration to attempt to establish mutually satisfactory decision dates. They should make their final choice at the earliest practicable date.

Acceptance of an employment offer should be made in good faith and with the sincere intention to honor the commitment.

5

EMPLOYMENT AGENCIES

Get the most out of agencies by knowing what to expect and what to watch out for

Employment agencies can be helpful partners when you are looking for a job. I found two of my jobs as a recruiter by going through employment agencies.

There are many good agencies, but others have a poor reputation — and they've earned it. Job hunters can tell horror stories about agencies. More than one candidate has been shocked to learn that an agency counselor has made a good, strong pitch about the candidate's talent — to the candidate's current boss.

Employers have complaints about agencies, too. The most common complaint is that some agencies do a terrible job of screening potential employees. They send an employer anyone who doesn't have three heads. An agency might send a chemical engineer out to interview for a job in electrical engineering, or a 40-year-old executive making $45,000 a year out to interview for an entry level job that pays $11,000 a year. Employers don't like to deal with a procession of people who aren't even close to the job specifications. Nor do candidates like being sent on wild goose chases. A $45,000-a-year executive sent out for an entry level job will really be frosted.

Employment agencies vary considerably in size and style. Some are one- or two-person operations; others have huge staffs. Some agencies are quartered in Spartan cubbyholes, while others are professionally decorated, comfortable places where each counselor has an office

59

with a door that actually closes. Still others bustle like Ellis Island at the turn of the century. When you walk in, you see an acre of desks, all crammed together. Telephones are constantly ringing, and counselors are hunched over phones looking as if they're trying to avoid being overheard by fellow counselors at nearby desks. You might even run across a touch of Hippodrome; one agency used to have a big ship's bell in the middle of the room. Whenever they placed a client in a job, they rang the bell.

Some agencies are stable, reliable organizations with a sincere interest in serving candidates and employers. Others are fast-buck operations interested only in peddling flesh any way they can. Quality varies broadly even among outlets of the same national agency. An outlet in one town might be excellent, while an outlet in a city 50 miles away might be awful.

Employers and the Agencies

Why do employers use employment agencies?

One reason is that they know that a lot of good people who want to change jobs work only through agencies.

Also, many employers feel that it can be better to work through a good agency than to add one or two staff people to their personnel department.

Furthermore, companies know that employment agencies can provide them with candidates who otherwise wouldn't consider their company. A candidate for an advertising copywriting job, for instance, might have several companies in mind that he would like to work for. He might not know that the XYZ Corporation exists. Or he might not have any interest in XYZ, and if he sees XYZ advertising in the paper for a copywriter, he might decide, "Oh, I guess I wouldn't want to work there." The employment agency counselor might tell such a candidate, "Say, XYZ is looking for a copywwriter. Good starting salary, not much commuting. Would you be interested?" When the candidate seems hesitant, the counselor can sell the company a little more: "We placed two people out there last year, an accountant and an engineer. Both are happy. XYZ management is progressive, and consequently, the company is growing. Its employee benefit program is one of the best in the state. You can't go wrong out there." And the company might gain a valuable employee that they otherwise wouldn't have had a chance to interview.

Most personnel departments work exclusively with one or two people in one or two agencies. When I was a recruiter, I dealt only with two agencies, one national and one local. I knew the people there, and I was able to say, "Don't send me any junk. When I ask for an accountant with two years' experience, that's just what I want." Once I got that point across, I could give the agents some leeway: I'd say, "I'll trust your judgment. If you want to monkey around with the experience level a bit, fine. Just don't send me any junk." It takes a long time for a recruiter to build a solid relationship with an agency. But when it does happen, the recruiter is going to be happy and the agency is going to make quite a bit of money.

Using an Agency

Agencies offer many advantages to the job seeker, too. Getting a job through an agency can be fast and efficient, an excellent way for busy people to look for a better job. You might wait six months for the right phone call, but the first time you go out on an interview, there's a good chance that you will get hired.

Ruth Dugan, who has operated two employment agencies, offers sound rationale for dealing with agencies:

> When you're employed but looking, opportunity is a strange thing. You never know when or where it may come to you.

You may have a stockbroker who watches the market for you and tells you when to buy or sell. His advice will increase your holdings.

You may have an accountant to help you prepare your tax reports. His advice and knowledge will help you retain a greater share of your holdings.

You may have a real estate agent who can find the house or property you want or assist you in selling. His advice and knowledge will make you money.

And when it comes to your job, your career, you can also profit by using an agent. Just as literary agents help writers find new markets or talent agents help entertainers get better jobs at better pay, so an employment agent can help you with your career.

You do not have to be out of work or actively seeking employment to need an agent. Timing is all-important: the job that is right for you and your career may not be available when circumstances have compelled you to seek new employment. Even if you are somewhat happily employed, an employment agent can at least make you the master of your own fate, of your own career. If there is a better opportunity, a more challenging position, a chance for greater personal advancement, he can keep you briefed and up-to-date as to what, with whom, where, and for how much. It costs nothing to listen, and it may cost a lot not to know.

Further, the discretion of a confidential employment agent is invaluable. Many employers regard the very fact that an employee is "looking" as grounds for dismissal or, at least, curtailment of plans for the person's advancement. As unrealistic and unreasonable as this attitude is, it must often be dealt with. It is not unfair to your present employer if you have an agent to keep you informed of other employment opportunities. Unless he owns the business, he probably has his own agent.

While he won't always admit it, every employer is keenly aware that a talented employee's first responsibility is to his own career. With the most specialized talent, when a person's initial job is accomplished, his choices become very narrow. He can abandon his specialization and attempt to assume more diverse responsibilities in the company he is with or he must seek another company for which his advanced specialization and experience are again valuable. Having an alert agent is a career necessity for such a person.

When you're unemployed, Ms. Dugan suggests the following:

When you have quit a job, been laid off or axed off, you find yourself in an emotionally charged situation. At such times, an objective third party who can realistically present your credentials to prospective employers can mean the difference between prompt and satisfying reemployment or the ordeal of taking whatever is available or going unemployed until something comes up.

When a job and a person do not match, the fixing of blame is unnecessary and destructive. The employers blame the employees, who blame the employers — none of which gets jobs productively filled. Unless an employee has been dismissed for mental imbalance, alcoholism, theft, immoral behavior, or some such, any animosity between an employee and his former employer can often be resolved by a knowing agent sufficiently so that a reasonable reference can be obtained to satisfy a new employer. And when your self-confidence is at low-ebb, it is far better to have someone else who knows your field and knows your qualifications and employment possibilities call through the companies who might be interested in hiring you, talking to the people in those companies who would be making the decisions concerning your employment. Such a person can listen objectively to the many turndowns and rejections without becoming discouraged, knowing that it generally takes about 20 presentations to get one send-out, and between 6 and 10 send-outs to get a placement. And your agent can be counted up to present you in terms of past *accomplishment* and future *potential* rather than your most recent difficulties.

Where to Go

Picking the one agency in any locality that could best serve you would be like roulette. Asking around probably wouldn't help much. There aren't many people who are knowledgeable about the quality of various employment agencies.

One fruitful method might be to get last Sunday's newspaper, turn to the employment agency section, and see which agency is doing the most advertising. The advertising volume indicates what kind of traffic an agency is getting, and traffic can be one indication of success. But some bad agencies deal with a lot of people, so I wouldn't make volume my sole criterion. I might go to one or two cubbyholes; some very talented professionals in any business prefer Spartan surroundings to exterior trappings of prosperity.

I would pick out half a dozen agencies.

An agency will frequently encourage candidates to sign up only at that one agency. The counselor will say, "We cover this whole city, and you don't have to register with anybody else." That's nonsense. That agency probably does cover the whole city, but you don't know how well your counselor covers the city. You might get a very good counselor who does, indeed, have a lock on your field all over the city. But you can also draw a counselor who doesn't have the terrain blanketed. Counselors are quite reluctant to let Jack, at the next desk, help on your placement because if Jack places you, Jack collects the fee.

You should let each agency know that you are registering at several places. Then they'll know they have competition.

> **TIP:** If you live in San Francisco and want a job in Albuquerque, you're best off dealing with an agency in Albuquerque. A lot of agencies will tell you that they're part of a national force, and indeed they are. But the profit for the agency in your home town on an out-of-town placement is small. What the agency usually does is ship your resume to an affiliate in Albuquerque. Then, if that agency finds you a job in Albuquerque, the two agencies split the fee 80/20 — 80 percent for Albuquerque, 20 percent for San Francisco. That 20 percent is so low that the San Francisco agency is not going to spend much time trying to peddle you in Albuquerque. So it probably would be worth the time and money for you to go to Albuquerque and stop in at agencies there. After they meet you, they know the local employers they could recommend you to because of a face-to-face meeting. And they get the whole fee, so they're going to work at it.

When you go to the employment agency, you should dress just as you would for a job interview with a recruiter. The counselor at the agency will be making the same kind of screening decision a recruiter does. He or she will be measuring you, calculating how well he can place you (and how big a fee he or she can collect).

At the agency's office, the receptionist probably will direct you to a counselor who specializes in your field.

Good agencies have specialists who have been in industry. They know people and they know the jobs.

The counselor will interview you. He will review your resume and probably will ask you some additional questions. There is one major difference between an interview with a recruiter and an employment counselor — the counselor is your agent. If he is any good, he can give you advice about how you are dressed and how you handle yourself in an interview.

Sometimes his criticism can be brutal, but that's no time for you to be sensitive or defensive. The head of one agency said that some job seekers don't want to open up to a counselor. He said that when a counselor asks, "Why were you fired?" the job seeker will say, "I'll tell a potential employer why, but I won't tell you." That's silly. As the agency head says, "You should spill your guts to counselors. Tell them your innermost thoughts." The counselor is on your side. He wants to place you, and he will do anything he can to increase your marketability.

Ruth Dugan offers some insights on what to look for in a counselor:

> You will want your agent to be a salesman. He must be able to see your professional competence in a competitive market. His intelligent enthusiasm, thoroughness, persistence, and high degree of personal integrity are foremost qualities of value to you when you choose him as your representative.

Ms. Dugan also mentions several things to watch out for:

> Agents are people, too, and they have trouble with their jobs like everybody. Such troubles, however, may be catastrophic to your career if you depend upon an unreliable agent. You won't have access to an agent's placement record so you won't be able to determine his success or failure that way, but you *will* have a front seat in watching how he rationalizes his unsuccess during your own interview with him.
>
> If he counsels you to lie, his game is something other than professional longevity and the best possible situation for both employer and applicant. Steer clear of him.
>
> If he wants you to interview for jobs in another counselor's area and will not permit you to interview with other counselors within the agency, he is hiding his inadequacy to service his own area properly. Agency owners regard such activity as a syndrome of failure in a counselor and mark such an agent as being not long for the employment business.
>
> A counselor infected with the "Perfect Marriage Syndrome" shows a personal arrogance to applicants when they wish to change their line of work or product area. He will play god, sending you only to jobs on a level with your past accomplishments, for which you are currently overqualified and which offer you no potential. When he should be asking only if you can do the job, he will insist that you must have already *done* the job. Applicant beware.
>
> The "Well-Organized Syndrome" is evident when a counselor wastes days, weeks, and

months organizing his desk, his files, his presentations, promising that as soon as he gets
everything ready he will find you a job. Don't
wait. He will probably have to find himself a
job first.

The "Something Other Than a Send-Out
Syndrome" will become apparent to you when
the counselor sets you to taking endless tests or
writing resumes *before* he has presented you to
potential employers. Some employers will want
an applicant to bring a resume to the first
interview and will want their people pretested,
but this is rare. Extensive mailings of resumes
do not get people interviews, nor do batteries of
test scores. Such an agent is *trying* to disqualify
you rather than find what you can do best. You
don't need him.

Laziness in an agent is hopeless. If your
agent is lethargic, you should seek another
agent — energetically.

If the agency has openings, the counselor will send you
out for interviews — and then you're into the game with
the corporate recruiter or manager.

If you have strong indications that your counselor isn't
putting forth much effort for you, prod him. If that doesn't
work, tell him that if he doesn't get busy, you will complain to his boss and ask for another counselor. That
probably will get results.

I had a stockbroker who ignored me. The market could
drop a hundred points, and I wouldn't hear from him. I
complained to the head of the brokerage and got a new
broker. The new broker pays attention to me because he
knows how he got me. Similarly, if you complain about an
employment agency counselor and get a new one, the new
one is going to pay attention to you.

When you deal with employment agencies, you should
always hold up your end of the deal. If an agency sets up

an interview for you, you must not stand the employer up. You should be there unless it is impossible. If you can't make it, you should give as much notice as you can to the agency and the employer. If you are still on the job market and you fail to show up for an interview, you certainly have blown your relationship with the employment agency — and you have tarnished the agency's relationship with the employer.

An agency head tells of some of the frustrations that agencies endure. On any given morning, the agency might send six candidates out for interviews. Candidate number one's car breaks down. Candidate number two forgets about the interview. The company that was to interview candidate number three calls and reports that they have to cancel the job order because of orders from headquarters. Candidate number four can't find the company's plant and misses the interview. Candidate number five took another job two days after the interview was set up and hasn't notified the agency, so he's a no-show. Candidate number six kept the appointment but didn't like the job. That makes for a bad day. But later in the day a corporate recruiter might call and say, "You know that designer you sent over three weeks ago? This afternoon we hired him."

> **TIP:** If you are a college graduate or if you are in a field that requires special education, such as nursing or aviation, or if you don't have a degree but have significant professional experience, it is unlikely that you will pay the employment agent's fee. The practice of new employees paying the agency fee when they get a professional job is becoming passé. Most employers will pay the fee, which is usually between 10 percent and 20 percent of the salary for the first year. Occasionally you will find an employer who won't pay the fee, or will split it, or will pay half now and half in six months or

70

any other weird combination. Maybe the job is attractive enough that you will want to come up with the money. It is unlikely you will run into an employer who will refuse to pay the fee, and remember, if you do, it is negotiable, and you probably have the advantage — the employer has selected you, and agency fees, though steep, are a very small part of the total employment cost.

Some agencies will require you to sign a contract that specifies that if the employer won't pay the fee for you, you must pay. I would sign the contract, but I would tell the agency that I refuse to pay a fee and would tell them not to send me to any companies that won't pay it. I would further tell the agency that under no circumstances would I accept any job where I would have to pay the fee. (This is my personal attitude toward employment agency fees. I am sure it decreases my opportunities slightly. You may want to keep all options open.)

Many people who do not have degrees or who are applying for such jobs as secretary or assembly line worker are more likely to be asked to pay their own fees.

Many people suspect that agencies list nonexistent jobs in newspaper ads as come-ons. Most states have laws that require an agency to have a bona fide order for any job it advertises. Government inspectors can investigate at any time. So while there may be a few phony come-ons, most of the jobs are real. Although that $28,000 dream job listed in the ad might be in North Vietnam, it probably does exist. However, a lot of the claims about the jobs — including salary — are inflated.

Your present boss might fire you if he finds out you're looking for a job. If you mail out a bunch of resumes on your own, the word could get back to your boss. There's a grapevine in every industry. The employment agency can prevent that by coding your resume. Instead of being advertised as Barbara Keller, you go out as No. 9604789. And the name of your present employer can be kept secret, too.

It's a good idea to remind the agency not to send your resume to your present employer. Such blunders have been made.

Executive Search Firms

Employment agencies look for jobs.

Executive search firms look for people.

Search firms usually are hired to find executives and highly skilled, highly paid employees.

A company will call a search firm and say, "We need an executive with experience in a company that makes left-handed monkey-wrenches." The search agent probably will meet with the company's recruiter, the head of the department where the opening is, or with other executives to learn the job specifications. Then the game's afoot. The agent goes out and starts stalking the market for candidates.

Unlike employment agencies, search firms get their money in advance. Sometimes the entire fee is paid in advance; sometimes part is paid in advance and part when a prospect accepts the job. The minimum usually is about 20 percent of the first year's pay plus a percentage of such extras as bonuses. Fees can go as high as more than the annual salary.

Employers consider search firms helpful for several reasons. Sometimes the employer simply doesn't know where to turn for a certain type of executive or specialist.

The marketplace can be mysterious, and employers know that executive search firms can cut through some of the mystery. For example, a major oil company might want a vice-president of marketing. The company's executives know the marketing vice-presidents of their strongest competitors and might not like them, or they might think they aren't very good. So they don't know where to go. A search firm might come up with a good candidate from the cosmetics industry.

Search firms can also help a company pull discreet raids on other companies. Although talent raids are severely frowned upon in business, just about any company will raid. But they don't want to advertise the fact. Search firms can shroud a raid in anonymity — not total anonymity, for when a search firm raids Company A to find a vice-president for Company B, Company A will know what happened. But if Company B conducts its own search, everyone they talk to, including all the people they contact and decide they don't want and all the people who decide they aren't interested in the job, will know that a raid is on. And they can spread the word.

Twenty years ago, when I was the recruiter for a company in Pennsylvania, we hired a search firm to find us a treasurer. We wanted strict anonymity, and the searcher came up with a good candidate who also wanted absolute secrecy, apparently because he feared that talking with another company would jeopardize his existing job or his standing in the company.

So the agent from the search firm set up a meeting involving me, the president of my company, and the candidate in a ski lodge that was closed for the summer. The lodge was 200 miles from our plant and probably was a long way from the candidate's place of business.

The search agent introduced us. To the candidate he said, "This is the president of the interested company and this is the personnel director." To us, he said, "This is a man who has credentials that we think will interest you." No names were used.

We brought all sorts of information about our company for him to look over. It was typed on bond paper with no letterhead. It included vague information about our product and the financial standing of our company and a very general description of the plant locale.

He brought similarly veiled information about himself. His resume said he was "most recently employed by a Fortune 500 company" and that he had graduated from a big state university.

We talked for most of the day, and we found him to be an impressive candidate. We made an offer. He declined. And that was that.

To this day I don't know his name, and I assume he doesn't know mine.

The search agent's chief commodity is names. Sometimes he can get them by placing a newspaper ad, as an employer would. But if newspaper advertising fails to produce the kind of candidate he wants, he might start working the phone. A clever search agent with a telephone is like a maestro with a Stradivarius.

I once watched a search agent work on an order to produce some people steeped in highly specialized technical knowledge. The company told him the kind of person they wanted probably could be found working for one particular giant corporation in the East.

The agent needed names. So he got on the phone and called the company.

The first call was to the main switchboard. He asked the company operator to connect him to the office of the head of the mechanical engineering department. Naturally the man's secretary answered the phone by saying "Mr. Anderson's office." The agent wrote down "Anderson" on the top of an organizational chart he was starting to construct. Then he told the secretary, "I'm from down in maintenance. Somebody up there is complaining about the air-conditioning. I don't think it was Mr. Anderson. I think it was one of his assistants."

"Mr. Schwartz?" asked the secretary.

"No, I don't think so."

"Mr. Cassidy?"

"No, it wasn't him."

"Then it must have been Mr. Fowler," she said.

"Yeah," he said, "I think that's who it was. I'll call his office." And the agent wrote on the second tier of his chart "Schwartz," "Cassidy," "Fowler."

Then a half-hour later, he called Schwartz's office and worked the same dodge on his secretary. Within a day he had the entire department charted. He probably got every name in the department.

The next step was to go through the local city directory. City directories list people's occupations and their employers, so all he had to do was find out which Fowler, Schwartz, Cassidy, etc., worked in the mechanical engineering department at that company. Then he had the full names and the phone numbers. Several people were eventually hired, and the agent had quite a pay day.

Sometimes search agents don't have to go through all that rigamarole to get names. If an agent can get his hands on a company directory, he's got it made. Many a company directory has been bought by a search agent from a disgruntled or greedy employee.

Lists of people who attend trade conventions can also be helpful.

If a Search Agent Calls You

A search agent presents himself to a prospective candidate in a fairly straightforward way. The agent will identify himself. He may or may not tell you the name of the company he is representing. He probably will take up the first few minutes of the conversation describing the job to you. Then he will ask if you are interested. If not, that's as far as it goes (although he may ask you if you know anyone else who might be good for the job).

If you do express interest, you go right into an interview situation with the agent. He might ask you a few basic questions about yourself, and he might start to develop a resume on you as you talk.

You might find that because of something in your background or because you lack some credential, the search agent will tell you he has decided he doesn't want to go any further with you. If he does decide to continue with you, he probably will set up an interview with officials from the company.

If the search agent does set up an interview, you can be fairly certain that he has given the company a pitch about what a good candidate you are. He wants the deal to go through. When you go into an introduction with the recommendation of a high-priced search agent, you go in bursting with power.

Should You List with Search Firms?

Does it pay for you, a candidate, to register with an executive search firm? It can. The firm just might have an order that you fit. But the primary function of a search firm is to find people for jobs, not jobs for people. So if you go into a search firm and ask them what they have for you, don't be surprised if they don't produce a long list of tempting jobs in your field.

State Employment Services

All job hunters, whether experienced or entry level, should register with their state employment service. The service is free to both the candidate and the employer. Most employers feel that state employment services are only effective in filling entry level, lower level, or blue collar jobs, but occasionally they get interesting listings at higher levels. Some state employment services can be excellent job sources at all levels.

Item E

Geography Lesson

You do not get hired in the employment lobby. That simple statement may seem outrageously obvious, but many job seekers do not consider its significance.

Some people think that if they go to company head-quarters and leave their resume with the personnel manager's receptionist, they have really accomplished something. They haven't gained a whit. Hand-carrying a resume to a receptionist is no better than mailing it in.

Some people feel that they have had an interview if the personnel manager came out into the lobby, greeted them, collected their resume, and politely dismissed them. They probably lost the job in the lobby.

If the personnel manager comes out in the lobby, he probably is protecting his den and his time from you. For some reason he has decided that talking to you is not worth his time and that the quickest way to get rid of you is to tell you he will take your resume, look it over, and get in touch with you. Do not surrender your resume to him in the lobby. If it looks as if he is not going to invite you into his office, ask for an appointment. If you get an appointment, shove your resume back in your pocket and clear out. If he seems reluctant to give you an appointment, say something like, "Well, if you can spare a few minutes, I'd like to talk with you briefly in your office."

You have to make it clear that you are not going to settle for a meaningless encounter in the lobby.

People do not do business in lobbies. Not even lobbyists. The lobby is poor terrain for the job seeker. It's the badlands. The fertile valleys are the personnel manager's office and beyond.

MISSIONARY WORK

Getting hired by getting the interview

Making cold calls on employers, either by sending your resume, or phoning, or dropping in off the street, is called missionary work. Missionary work can be discouraging when you need a job and don't have one. Every setback is a crunching blow to your ego, and several weeks of continuous refusals can pummel even the most confident psyche into mush.

Missionary work can be particularly difficult for new college graduates because many employers fill their entry level jobs through on-campus recruiting. Also, new graduates doing missionary work have to compete with experienced people who are probably more at ease in the professional world. The experienced person can talk more knowledgeably about the field and can point to his or her professional accomplishments.

But for the college graduate who has failed to connect through the college placement center and has no contacts to take advantage of, missionary work is about all that's left. People in that situation should hit the street hard.

When you do missionary work from the comfortable vantage point of a secure job, it's fun. It's like looking for better fruit in somebody else's orchard. When you already have a job, you are in a much stronger bargaining position. If you have a good reputation in your field, you can be highly attractive to an organization, and that is real leverage.

77

No matter what your situation, you can succeed at missionary work if you get out and do it and if you do it right.

Where to Look

Highly skilled, heavily experienced managers and other specialists have the entire world as their hunting ground when they do missionary work. A sales manager who has sent the line on his company sales graph through the fluorescent lights on the ceiling has a ticket to almost any corporation. A successful department store buyer in Cincinnati would be able to spark interest from good stores in New York or Miami.

But new high school and college graduates and people with easy-to-come-by skills are more limited. Their home town or state can be their oyster, but the rest of the world is probably going to be their clam — slammed shut. If you fall into one of these categories, the closer to home you look, the better your chances are. A junior accountant or a new liberal arts graduate could blanket New York with resumes and would undoubtedly receive a pile of "area letters," which say, "If you're ever in the area, stop in and see us." They're not going to fly you in to look you over when they can find plenty of people with your qualifications in their own territory.

If you are absolutely determined to get a job in Boston or Washington or San Francisco, your best bet is to go there. Then start looking.

When to Look

The best time to apply for a job is 10 in the morning. If you don't get in right away, you have a good shot at getting in before noon because the personnel manager likes to clean out the lobby before lunch. The second best time is about 3 in the afternoon; the manager probably will sweep the lobby again before going home.

Monday mornings and Friday afternoons are poor times to apply; a manager spends Monday morning putting out the fires that started over the weekend; on Friday afternoon everybody is sick of working and is bearing down to get out early.

Mornings are generally better than afternoons. People are a lot fresher and in better spirits in the morning. By afternoon they're dragging — or are out on the golf course or tennis court.

Holiday seasons — particularly from Thanksgiving to Christmas — are poor times to apply. Often the personnel manager, aware that there won't be much hiring from mid-November through New Year's, will take a vacation then. Sometimes personnel managers will all but shut down their hiring setups around November 15 and won't resume until after the first of the year. One reason that little hiring is done in the last month of the year is money: there are six paid days off in the last five weeks of the year. It would be expensive to hire a batch of new people and pay them for all that time off. The smart recruiter who gets a request from a line manager for a new employee will try to persuade the manager to put it off until the first of the year.

Also it is rather difficult to hire people after November 15. People are reluctant to relocate then. It is even difficult to get them to come in for an interview. Their kids are involved in holiday activities — Christmas plays at school and Sunday school pageants — and the adults are getting into a round of holiday partying that sets in about December 5. Another reason that people want to stay put until the new year is that they don't want to get cut out of Christmas and year-end bonuses.

That month and a half of stagnation results in a rich recruiting season in January. The employment office has been on the shelf for six weeks, so openings that otherwise would have been filled have piled up. Also, the turnover at other companies in January is high. People disappointed in Christmas bonuses feel they have been cheated and they want out. Many companies put their reorganization plans into effect on January 1. In every reorganization, there are winners and losers, and a lot of the losers are strong, competent employees who have fallen victim to company politics. Passed over or shoved aside, they want to move on.

The bullish job market continues through February, then cools off until May.

People don't like to pull their kids out of a school in the middle of a semester. So they wait until May, when the school year is almost over, to start looking around. The market stays strong through most of the summer. Then it cools off again in September. By October it drops off quickly, and in mid-November it collapses.

Meeting the Enemy

The same principle that applies to answering a newspaper ad applies to missionary work: don't send a resume; don't phone. Go to the company's personnel department. And when you do, the first person you meet is your enemy: the receptionist.

The receptionist is important to you. She obviously cannot hire you, but she can prevent you from being hired. If you don't deal properly with the receptionist, you can lose the job in the lobby because she can send you packing without an interview.

The Receptionist

The receptionist is usually female, frequently a recent high school graduate, and generally put in the job because she is attractive and "nice."

If you make cold calls on several organizations, you will probably encounter two types of receptionists: company receptionists and employment lobby (or personnel department) receptionists. At a big company, you will probably run into both types.

The company receptionist is a traffic cop. She sits in the main lobby of the building, smiles at people as they come in, and shoots them as directly as possible to the person they want to see. Sometimes she runs the company switchboard. Usually — but not always — the company receptionist won't be much of an obstacle for you: you ask her where the personnel department is, and she tells you how to get there.

The employment lobby receptionist's job is different. She is an employee of the personnel department, and she usually does more than just staff a desk and give directions. Most of her time is spent doing clerical work for the department. But as far as you are concerned, the most important part of her job is to protect the busy personnel manager, or recruiter, from you — the job seeker. The recruiter doesn't want to talk to every job seeker who comes in; that would take up too much time. He would much rather review resumes and applications and then call in people whose resumes interest him. So he uses the receptionist as a buffer. I have worked as a receptionist, and that is exactly what I did — protect the boss. I have worked as a personnel manager, and for 13 years I hid behind the capable skirts of Verna Mae, Kathy, and Louise. But I have seen all of them successfully manipulated by job seekers, just as I was manipulated when I was a receptionist.

The job of both the company receptionist and the employment lobby receptionist can be frustrating:

• Nobody ever comes to visit the receptionist. Everyone who checks in with the company receptionist wants to see the purchasing agent, the sales manager, the personnel manager, the field service engineer, or some other company luminary. Nobody ever says, "Hi, Receptionist, I dropped in to do some business with you." The same is true for the employment lobby receptionist. People don't want to deal with her. They want to see someone who can hire them.

• Often the work station of the receptionist is outside the normal flow of work. It is inconvenient and sometimes impossible to get assignments to and from her.

• The receptionist operates alone, with little or no supervision, and nobody to confer with about problems.

• A receptionist, particularly a company receptionist, has no real power, and she receives almost no recognition. She is far from indispensable. The easiest absentee to replace is the company receptionist. Almost anyone who can read the company directory can do the job.

This combination of junior status, inconvenient geography, and loose control often means that she doesn't have enough to do. And that adds to her frustration. After a while she might try to *create* some importance for herself and her function:

• The company receptionist might try to regulate the flow of traffic coming into her lobby. She might, for example, tell certain salesmen to come only in the afternoon. Such bold action is rare, but it has happened.

• The employment lobby receptionist might take it upon herself to do some prescreening of job seekers.

Don't let yourself get screened out by a receptionist. Most receptionists do not understand the qualifications required for jobs. In fact, many don't even know what jobs are open.

A recruiter is reluctant to tell the personnel department receptionist about a job opening. If he told her, she might do some moonlight recruiting among her friends and relatives. The recruiter doesn't want to be forced into an interview with the receptionist's brother-in-law. Such an interview is always loaded against the recruiter. He knows that the receptionist has all but guaranteed the brother-in-law that he will get a job offer Also she's primed him with information about salary, hours, and the boss. What's more, the recruiter knows that if the brother-in-law gets hired, there will be a meeting every morning at the coffee machine that will have to be stopped. If he doesn't hire the brother-in-law, the receptionist goes into a snit and won't talk to anybody in the personnel department for a week, making herself unproductive and the atmosphere unpleasant. So the recruiter keeps the receptionist in the dark.

Beating the Receptionist

Occasionally a company receptionist will be an obstacle, particularly at a small company. Employment lobby receptionists generally will be the ones you have to beat. Usually it is you versus the personnel receptionist, one on one.

> **TIP:** Before you walk in off the street to apply for a job, you should find out the name of the person who screens for the job. If you answer an ad in the paper and the name of the person to whom you should send your resume is listed, you don't have a problem. If you are following up an ad that doesn't list the person's name or if you're making cold calls on companies, you should do some digging to find out. If you know people who work for the company, ask them. If not, you can call the company offices and ask the company operator the name of the personnel manager. Sometimes, as soon as you get the words "personnel manager" out of your mouth, the operator will put your call into the personnel department. You can head that off. As soon as the operator answers and says, "ABC Company," you can say, "I don't want to talk to the personnel department, I just want to know the

name of the personnel manager." The operator will give you the name. If it's a huge company, you might want to call the personnel department and ask the receptionist the name of the person who screens for the kind of job you want. Then, when you go up against the receptionist, you can ask for the recruiter by name.

Beating the receptionist is easy if you have a plan and a lot of patience. You might also have to get tough. The scenario might go something like this:

You: Good morning. My name is John King. I'd like to see Mr. Savage.

Receptionist: Do you have an appointment?

You: No. But I want to talk to him about a sales job. I have qualifications he'll be interested in.

Receptionist: Well, I'm sorry, Mr. Savage works only by appointment.

You: Fine. May I have an appointment? I'm free all day. (If the receptionist gives you an appointment, you have won your battle, and you should leave and return to keep the scheduled appointment. Don't leave your resume with the receptionist or you may return for your appointment only to learn that Savage "reviewed your background," decided that you don't fit, and canceled your appointment.)

Many receptionists won't give you an appointment. The boss will be mad if the receptionist starts programing his days for him. Instead of giving you an appointment, she will probably say something like, "Mr. Savage is very busy this morning. Why don't you leave your resume with me, and I'll see that he gets it." Remember, the personnel manager would rather review you on paper than talk to you. You, of course, should not part with your resume at this point.

Your response should be something like: "I'm not in a hurry, I'll wait until he can see me." (You can embellish that response by saying something like, "I'm not working today [maybe because you're unemployed, but this statement may cause the receptionist to think you have taken the day off], and I have traveled some distance to talk to Mr. Savage." [Maybe you've only come six blocks, but that's "some distance." If you've traveled a hundred miles, say you've traveled a hundred miles.] "If you don't mind," tell her, "I'll just wait until Mr. Savage can see me. And if you can help me get in to see him, I'd certainly appreciate it."

You have just done two important things:

• You asked the receptionist to help you, and that's very often just what she will do.

• More important, you have applied some pressure on her. You have let her know that she hasn't gotten rid of you. You will not go away.

Receptionists are constantly working for an empty lobby. The lobby is *their* territory, and strangers like you are trespassers. The receptionist resents your presence there, and there are reasons. Maybe she's into a fascinating magazine article and would feel uncomfortable reading in front of you. Maybe there's a department rule that she can't smoke when there's an outsider in the lobby, and she's dying for a cigarette.

The receptionist doesn't want you in her lobby. Yet there you sit. Doing nothing. You should not smoke. You should not read the magazines on the coffee table. You should do nothing that would interfere with the psych job you are going to do on the receptionist. Try staring at her. Nobody likes to be watched; it's like having somebody read over your shoulder. Staring will add to the pressure of your unwanted presence. It will make her uncomfortable and will decrease her home-turf advantage. Mix up your routine to keep her off balance. Act nervous. Pace. Ask her questions like, "What does his calendar look like?" Pour it on.

If you bug the receptionist enough, an interesting phenomenon might take place. She might start to bug Savage. And Savage will almost always eventually respond to such pressure for one of two reasons:

• You're upsetting his shop. To bring things back to normal, it looks as though he's going to have to see you.

• If Savage has been in the business long, he is afraid of most candidates and is terrified of *all* of the aggressive ones. Aggressive people usually have a weapon, and he doesn't know what yours is.

The skilled recruiter fears the candidate who might file an unfair employment practices claim against the company because no one would talk to him. He fears the candidate whose relatives might be stockholders, present employees, or customers.

One morning I was fat and happy, at my desk working away merrily, when the company president stormed in. He slammed the door and demanded, "Just what the hell do you do for a living?" It turned out that his daughter had been in to apply for work the day before. She was married, and neither I nor my receptionist responded to her married name. She sat in our lobby for close to an hour, then gave up and went home. Angry, she called Dad and complained. She heaped it on us by telling him she was surprised that nobody would see her because "nobody seemed very busy." Dad spent two hours disassembling me, and I think that the incident hurt me the next time I came up for a salary review.

Knowledgeable personnel officials live in fear of the employment lobby because it blows up regularly, and every explosion leaves another scar. All of the following have happened to me:

• A referral by a local union executive wasn't handled correctly. The union executive made life miserable for me.

• The niece of a long-time employee wasn't interviewed. The employee hollered at me.

• The son of a stockholder wasn't interviewed. The stockholder complained in a letter to the president, and, of course, I heard about it.

• The son of a major customer was turned down, and the customer threatened to take his business elsewhere.

You, the candidate, should capitalize on the recruiter's lobbyphobia.

After the receptionist has bugged Savage a few times and reminded him that you are still in the lobby, he may resort to a favorite recruiter stratagem: asking the receptionist to pick up your resume so he can give it a look before seeing you. The receptionist will come over to you and say, "May I have your resume, please? Mr. Savage would like to review it before he talks to you."

That sounds pretty good. It sounds as if you're going to get in. But don't fall for it. *Don't give it to her.* Unless your resume is exceptionally powerful, she will take it and will probably be back in less than five minutes saying, "Mr. Savage has reviewed your resume, and there doesn't seem to be anything for you now, but we will be happy to keep you on file, and if anything should come up in the future, we'll contact you." That, of course, is just a pleasant way of throwing you out. It means you have lost.

When the receptionist asks for your resume or application, smile and pleasantly say, "If you don't mind, I'd like to give this to Mr. Savage myself. There are some significant items in my background that need explaining, and I have a couple questions of my own. I need only a few minutes of his time, and I will be happy to wait until he can conveniently see me."

It has reached the point where the receptionist has to be an ogre to separate you from your resume. Most people don't like to become ogres. That goes double for receptionists because, after all, they're supposed to be specialists in pleasantry.

Savage has just shot his last arrow, and you now have him neatly boxed. The receptionist, clearly recognizing that she is now in the middle between you and Savage, might go back to him, without your resume, and say, "Mr. Savage, this man says he needs just a few minutes, and he really does seem pretty impressive. Will you be able to squeeze him in soon?" What she really thinks is that you're a big pain and she wants you out of her lobby. But notice how she has become your ally. The struggle is now between you and Savage. He knows that since you wouldn't give up your resume, he is dealing with a smooth, skilled job hunter.

The only other trap you have to avoid now is his coming out into the lobby and trying to give you a quick brush-off. You can foil that by forcing him to give you an appointment or asking to talk in his office.

So you should have your interview.

Won't the recruiter be angry at you for bullying his receptionist and forcing yourself on him? He might. But don't let that bother you. The receptionist is more irritated than the recruiter, and she can't hire you or at this point, turn you down. The recruiter may be irritated, but he's probably no fool. If he has an opening and if you are a good candidate, he won't turn you away. He knows that he might have to look a long time to find someone as good as you.

> **TIP:** You should soften the recruiter's irritation by beginning the interview with a brief but cordial apology for crashing in on him: "Mr. Savage, I'm sorry for bursting in on you like this, but I really am anxious to talk with you about working for ABC." If you don't serve up such an apology, your interview will not go as well.

NOTE: When you work such a routine on a receptionist, you should be firm, *but at all times be polite*. If you are loud or obnoxious, you won't impress anyone.

CAUTION: Of course, your encounter in an employment lobby might not go exactly according to the above scenario. It is your *attitude* that is most important. You have to realize that you might have to become an employment lobby guerrilla to get past the receptionist. But you also have to be flexible and alert for variations.

A young man who took my advice on dealing with the receptionist wrote me this letter:

Dear Mr. Stanat:

...I decided to take your advice. You were right about the receptionist being your enemy, as you will find out as my letter continues.

I completed an application for _____ Company. The application was fully completed. My appearance was neat. I wore a suit, shined shoes, clean hair and body, etc.

I gave the receptionist my application and asked to talk with the personnel manager. I was told they weren't hiring and no one would talk to me. I asked her if he would review my application that day. She said maybe they would. I told her I would be seated in case he would like to talk to me.

I sat for close to an hour when I saw the personnel manager pick up my application and take it with him to his office. I walked up to the desk and a different girl had taken the first girl's place. I told her I saw the personnel manager take the pile of applications. I asked her if she would call him and tell him I was in the office in case he would like to interview me. She asked me for my name and wrote it down. She started to pick up the receiver when the first girl came back and said, "No. I already told him we weren't hiring." I told them I would take a seat for a little longer in case he was impressed with my application.

As I was seated, I overhead the first girl say to the second girl, "We should call the police on this guy and have him arrested for loitering." I left then, as I didn't want to hassle with the police and it was 2:30 and I had to be to work by 3:00.

I thought her remark was disgusting because I wasn't harassing anyone. It was also rather embarrassing, as there were other people in the office.

I still think your [advice] was good and I will continue to follow your advice.

Signature

This man took a shot at it and lost. He might have won if he had done some things differently. Turning in the application was a mistake. But even then he wasn't out of the game. There were several situations he could have capitalized on. When the personnel manager picked up the stack of applications, the applicant could have gone over to the manager and said quietly (because there were other people in the lobby), "Mr. Smith, my application is in that pile and there are some things in it I would like to talk to you about. Also, I have a few questions. I have to be at work in a few minutes, but I'd sure appreciate it if I could talk to you in your office for a couple of minutes." That would have forced a face-to-face decision, and it might have worked. The odds are about 50-50.

He missed another chance when the receptionist got snotty and started talking about calling the cops. From his letter, he seemed genuinely concerned that the constabulary might have been summoned. Obviously this company, a well-known manufacturer of a consumable product, was not going to call the police to throw a possible employee out of their lobby. If they had, the guy really would have scored. It might have resulted in newspaper publicity and job offers from companies that were impressed by his aggressiveness.

When the receptionist got snotty, she gave him a perfect weapon. He could have gone home, checked around (perhaps in the city directory) and learned the home address of the chief executive of the company. Then he could have sent the chief executive a polite registered letter outlining the bad treatment he received from the receptionist. He would have had his interview.

Then there was a woman who made a stand in the lobby.

> The woman, a former nun, earned a degree in sociology, wanted to go into social work, but couldn't find a job. She was writing letters and sending resumes, but getting nowhere. Then I gave her a pitch on lobby tactics, and she went out and put them to work.
>
> She heard through the grapevine that there was an opening at a home for delinquent girls. She went to the home and ran into a receptionist.
>
> "May I see the director?" she asked.
>
> "I'm sorry; he's awfully busy today," she was told.
>
> "That's okay. I'll wait," the woman said.
>
> She sat there from 10 in the morning until 5 in the afternoon. At 5 the receptionist came over and said, "I told you nobody would see you today. I'm closing the office now. You'll have to leave."
>
> So she left. And came back at 9 the next morning.

Imagine the receptionist's thoughts: "My God, she's back!"

Everyone in the organization must have been talking about the dummy outside the director's office. Undoubtedly there was coffee room chatter, with the receptionist telling everyone, "That woman's back. She doesn't go to lunch. She doesn't go to the bathroom. She just sits there."

And it's a sure bet that anytime other employees saw the director they jabbed him about it, "Hey, Mike, when you gonna talk to the ding-a-ling in the lobby?"

About 10 o'clock, the director couldn't stand it any longer. He came out into the lobby and said to the woman, "Miss, I know that you were here all day yesterday, and I know you've been here since we opened this morning. But I can't possibly see you today."

And she smiled at him and said, "That's okay, I'll wait."

Exasperated, he said, "Come on in."

They went in. They talked. And at one o'clock that afternoon she started her new job.

The director *was* too busy to talk to the woman because he was shorthanded. Interviewing is a long, expensive, often nonproductive function. He didn't know whether the woman was any good or not, and he didn't want to take the time to find out because three days' work was piled up on his desk.

But she *forced* him to talk to her. He was probably furious when they went into his office. But how incredibly stupid it would have been to start to talk to that woman, discover she was just the candidate he wanted, and not hire her because he was irritated.

If that woman had allowed the receptionist or the director to stonewall her and take her resume, she probably would have received a form letter 10 days later saying, "If something comes up, we'll be in touch."

But she refused to lose the job in the lobby. Don't let a receptionist stonewall you. You should crash and jam until you are sitting across from the decision maker.

Does It Always Work?

Is "crashing" guaranteed to get you an interview every time? I don't think that any tactic works 100 percent of the time. There are some personnel people who simply will not see you without an appointment. But there also are a lot of recruiters who *say* they won't see anyone without an appointment and then cave in when pressured. Most of the time you should get your interview. If you do fail, try again at the next place.

I described the tactics for getting past the receptionist to a recruiter for a big manufacturing company, and he said, "If anybody did that in my office, I'd throw him out."

I said, "Would you really, Stan?"

He thought about it for a few seconds and said, "No, I guess I wouldn't. If anybody wanted to work for us that bad, I'd want to see them."

What does "the other side" think about such tactics? Do employers favor personal visits? Frank S. Endicott, Emeritus Director of Placement at Northwestern University, surveyed employers and published the results in the 1972 annual report, *Trends in Employment of College and University Graduates in Business and Industry* which is published and copyrighted by Northwestern University and its Placement Center. (Table 6-1).

In that survey, making cold calls is rated fifth out of six. Only 19 out of 126 respondents (16 percent) favor the idea of candidates walking in.

TABLE 6-1

Several questions concerning desirable procedure for making application were included in this year's [survey]. They are listed below. It should be noted that not all companies responded to every question. Nevertheless, a pattern seems to be clear. A procedure preferred by 80 percent of the companies is the letter enclosing a resume.

Procedures for Contacting the Company	Number of Company Responses	
	Yes	No
Write a brief letter giving fairly complete information about themselves.	80	53
Write a brief letter telling why they are interested in your company and enclosing a resume.	145	7
Telephone the personnel office for an appointment.	33	95
Seek an appointment with an executive not in personnel.	2	124
Come to the office, hoping to talk with someone about employment.	19	107
Have a professor, dean, or placement officer make a direct contact with your company in their behalf.	42	87

That is not surprising. The employers are upholding *their* system. If you act according to their preferences — sending a resume, writing a letter — you increase your chances of being *screened out*.

You Won't Always Have to Push

You won't have to go to war with a receptionist in every personnel office you visit. Several companies, including at least one giant of the petroleum industry, have an open-door policy. They automatically interview everyone who comes in.

Item F

Pull

Use pull. It gets big parts for marginal movie stars. It gets laws through Congress. It helps put multimillion dollar business deals across. And it can help you get a job. Pull is any force you can exert on the hiring process from inside the organization.

You might have more pull than you think. You don't have to be the niece of the chairman of the board to use connections to get a job. You don't even have to know an executive of the organization you want to work for. You have pull if you can get someone to recommend you to the right executive.

There are six kinds of pull, ranked unscientifically, that can help you get hired.

• **Pull based on blood relationship.** If your father or mother is the emperor or empress of the company, you're in. That's all there is to it. Other blood relationships aren't always a cinch. It depends on the company. If your uncle is a department manager, you might be a shoo-in. Then again, the company might have a policy against nepotism.

• **Pull based on business obligation.** That's how the whole political system works. Political volunteers spend months on campaign tedium. They're building up a storehouse of credit. When their candidate gets elected, they go to him when they want a law passed or when they want a government job. Patronage did not go out with Andrew Jackson, and it never will go out. Business works the same way. If you did something that advanced somebody's career, perhaps when you worked together at a different company, that person is obligated to you. It could be something major, such as helping someone land an important account or giving a person a tip that helped get a promotion. Or it could be something minor, such as helping somebody write a speech for a professional convention. When you are looking for a job, call in your debts.

• **Pull based on friendship.** Cronies help each other get jobs all the time. If you have a friend who can hire you for a job you want, take it. If you have a friend who can go to his boss and say, "I have a friend who would be perfect for the job," you have a strong ally. There is less pulling power with friendship than there is with a business debt because employees are a bit sheepish about saying, "I have a friend who...." But it can work.

• Pull based on professional respect. If you know that someone in a company knows that you are good, ask him to put in a word for you. Many people will do it because it will advance their own careers. Others will not do it because you would be competition.

• Pull based on a common bond. The hiring agent or some other influential employee in a company may have been in your fraternity, goes to your church, went to the same far-off university as you did, or comes from the same small town. People have allegiances to those things. You can appeal to a person's tribal instinct, which causes him to think, "He's one of my kind; therefore he must be okay. I'll hire him."

In *The Pyramid Climbers*, Vance Packard tells of one corporate recruiter who blatantly loaded up his company's junior management ranks with guys from his old college fraternity. Finally — but only after quite a while — top management made him start looking beyond his brotherhood.

• The pull of casual acquaintance. If you used to caddy for the president or the sales manager of a company you want to work for, go see him. Remind him that you used to caddy for him and tell him you want a job. If you met somebody at a party and if you think you impressed him, go see him when you want a job. This kind of pull is not nearly as strong as the other five, because there is no pressure on the other person. But it is worth a try.

The effectiveness of pull can be traced to the nature of the hiring process. Hiring is always a gamble. Therefore, executives welcome any development that can decrease the gamble. An executive's good impressions of you at some time other than when you were looking for a job or the recommendation of somebody inside the organization makes you less of a risk than an unknown applicant.

In most cases when you use pull, your first contact with the organization will be with somebody other than the recruiter. But in most big organizations you probably will be processed through the personnel department. A likely chronology would be:

• You tell a friend that you heard there is a good sales job open in the same company he sells for. You ask the friend if he would recommend you to his boss. If he agrees to make a pitch for you, ask him to report back to you after he makes the pitch.

• The friend recommends you to the boss and gets back to you with the boss' reaction.

• You call the boss and express your interest in the job.

• The boss either sets up a meeting with you or tells you to report to the personnel department.

• If he refers you to the personnel department, he calls the recruiter and tells him that you are coming in. He also tells the recruiter that you are strongly recommended by one of the people in his department.

So when you go in piggyback — riding on somebody's sponsorship or recommendation — you have a lot more power than if you come in cold. You don't have the job locked up, but you have a strong advantage. If the department head himself is your sponsor, you're extremely powerful when you deal with the recruiter. All you have to do is avoid major blunders.

The use of pull is a reversal of the normal process. Instead of the recruiter paving the way for you with a manager, a manager has paved the way for you with the recruiter. Recruiters vary in their reactions to a candidate with pull. Most probably resent it a little, for it is, after all, an infringement on their function. But, to a recruiter, a candidate with pull has a major redeeming aspect: if that candidate doesn't work out, it isn't the recruiter's fault. He can always say, "I didn't select that loser. The vice-president ordered me to put him to work."

Don't try to suggest that you have pull when you don't. Don't tell the recruiter, "I know Jim Hawkins on your board of directors," even when you do know Hawkins casually. Such name dropping will weaken, not strengthen, your position with the recruiter. He'll figure, "If he's so tight with Hawkins, why the hell isn't Hawkins sponsoring him?" If you have a good relationship with Hawkins, work through him. If you don't use him, don't mention him.

> **CAUTION:** When you use pull, be absolutely certain that you can do the job. And if you get the job, you must work extra hard to produce. The professional credibility of a friend or other connection is riding on your performance. So you must deliver.

7

THE INTERVIEW

Anticipate different kinds of interviews

The hiring process has not changed significantly since the time of King Solomon. If a vineyard owner wanted grape pickers, he held interviews at the village well. Hiring was then, and still is, a belly-to-belly, eyeball-to-eyeball decision.

As a recruiter, I never hired anyone I hadn't met. I've hired high-priced executives in airport bars, and I've hired shirtless construction workers on the site. I talked face to face with every last one.

The interview is the only critical act in the hiring process. No talk, no job. Too many candidates think it is the recruiter's responsibility to make the interview happen. It's not. It's *your* responsibility.

That is true in almost every situation.

When you answer an ad in a newspaper or trade publication, you can't be content to mail in a resume. You must force the interview.

When you go through an employment agency, *you*, through your agent, are the prime mover in arranging your interview.

When you go through the campus placement center, it is *you* who must sign up for an interview with the recruiter. Otherwise he doesn't know you exist.

When you do missionary work, it is imperative that *you* get your body *across the desk* from the recruiter. Anything short of that will not get you a job.

Any obstacle between you and an interview with the decision maker is an obstacle between you and the job. So, as previous chapters have shown, you have to cut through any obstacles.

Once you get your interview, your next tactical objective is to convince the recruiter that you are the person for the job. To do that, you have to get four ideas across to him: that you are *competent*, that you are *intelligent*, that you are *honest*, that you are *likable*.

Countless academic researchers in countless universities have surveyed countless employers on what qualities they want and don't want in the people they hire. The responses have been counted, charted, measured, plotted, interpreted, codified, quantified, and deified. And, surprise! Employers prefer positive qualities to negative qualities. You can systematically go through the dictionary and, nearly every time you come to a noun or an adjective involving a personal trait, can judge instantly whether or not that would appeal to an employer: active, adaptable, aggressive, ambitious — employers are buying that; affected, abrasive, antagonistic, asinine — no sale.

Put all the negative traits together into a composite portrait, and you come up with a combination of Attila the Hun, Frankenstein's monster, the Bitch of Buchenwald, and the village idiot. The positive traits add up to a composite of Winston Churchill, Albert Einstein, Florence Nightingale, and the Venerable Bede.

But you don't have to study a long list of personality traits and characteristics to make sure you can convince the recruiter that you have most of the good ones and few of the bad. If you can convince the recruiter that you're competent, honest, likable, and intelligent, you've picked up most of the others along the way.

• Competence encompasses everything it takes to do the job: the right background and credentials, natural ability, reliability, the right amount of aggressiveness for the job, and the proper appearance and attitude. It also includes such traits as ability to work under pressure and decisiveness. The quality of your resume and the testimony of the people you use as references are important factors in convincing the recruiter that you are competent.

• Honesty is essential. It would be naive to suggest that there are not employers who would expect you to cheat someone else. But no employer is going to hire you if he thinks you might cheat or deceive him. The recruiter is not going to have anything to do with anyone who comes off as shifty. Never lie in a job interview. Not only is it foul, but you can also get caught. And if you get caught, you won't get hired. What if you got fired from your last job for stealing? Well, you're in trouble. But your best bet is to be forthright about it. It will certainly keep you from getting many jobs, but there are plenty of people in business who strongly believe that anybody deserves a second chance — and they are willing to back up that belief by hiring you.

• Intelligence is required for almost any job. Would you hire a stupid coal miner? No. One foolish action underground could jeopardize the lives of hundreds of people. The recruiter measures your intelligence according to how articulate, thoughtful, persuasive, and agreeable you are in answering his questions and asking him your questions.

• Likability is crucial. If you are an obnoxious, disagreeable, argumentative show-off, you should suppress your basic nature. That shouldn't be too hard to do for only a half-hour interview.

Your general demeanor throughout the interview will be what the recruiter will rely on most heavily in determining whether or not you measure up in competence, honesty, intelligence, and likability.

Keep this list of job interview "dos" and "don'ts" in mind. A good point to remember as you read the list is that no single do will get you the job. But any one of the don'ts could disqualify you.

Don'ts

Don't be late. In fact, plan to be 10 to 15 minutes early for any scheduled interview. If you are late or arrive just in the nick of time, the interviewer will start to wonder how prompt you might be after you start to work.

Don't wear your outer clothes into an interview. Take any kind of overcoat or topcoat off. Take rubber boots off and leave them in the employment lobby. Wearing those into an interview gives the impression that you are anxious to leave.

Don't sit down until you are asked. Don't worry about this. The recruiter won't make you stand, but if you move quickly to your chair and sit down, you will appear forward.

Don't have anything in your mouth except your teeth — no gum, no candies, no breath mints; in fact, don't smoke during the first interview; it is distracting to everyone.

Don't lean on or put your elbows on the interviewer's desk. Sit back in your chair, so the interviewer can see more of you. Sit erect.

Don't wear sunglasses into an interview, and if you don't wear your eyeglasses all the time, don't park them on top of your head (some candidates actually do that). Take them off and put them in your purse or pocket.

Don't carry an oversized handbag even if it is fashionable. Carry a bag that is smaller and more manageable. Put it on the floor during the interview, or hold it on your lap. Never place it on the interviewer's desk.

Don't have unusually long fingernails. This applies to men as well as women. Really long fingernails could indicate that you haven't really worked in a while — even office chores cause broken, and therefore shorter, fingernails.

Don't show your nervousness by drumming your fingers, swinging your leg, or cracking your knuckles. Men: don't have any loose change in your pocket — most of us tend to jingle it when we are nervous. (You really shouldn't have your hands in your pockets in the first place.)

Don't keep adjusting your clothes.

Don't fiddle with your hair.

Don't compare this recruiter's office with others that you have seen. The recruiter might decide that you have seen the inside of too many employment offices, including his.

Don't pick up anything from the recruiter's desk unless you are invited to do so.

Don't listen in on any phone calls the recruiter may receive while you are with him. Do your best to "tune out." After such a phone call, don't comment on something he said or ask a question about the conversation.

Don't stand if someone else (man or woman) enters the recruiter's office. Keep your chair and don't say anything to the visitor unless you are spoken to first. If the recruiter introduces you to the person who came in, then you can stand.

Don't inspect or read documents on the recruiter's desk.

Don't call the recruiter "sir" or "ma'am" too much. Respect is mandatory, but don't go overboard.

Don't overuse the interviewer's name. Too much Dale Carnegieism is annoying.

Don't be a jokester. Wisecracks and laughter can come later. Be pleasant, but remember that the interviewing process is formal and serious. An overly lighthearted approach will cause the interviewer to question the seriousness of your purpose.

Don't give one- and two-word answers. The recruiter is trying to get to know you. Talk to him. If you go into a shell, you probably won't be hired.

Don't hog the conversation. Answer the questions thoroughly, but don't drone on forever.

Don't interrupt. That's rude in a saloon, and it is inexcusable in an interviewing situation.

Don't use profanity, even if the recruiter does. It can't possibly help your image.

Don't use a lot of slang.

Don't gush. You can be pleasant without being syrupy.

Don't say "you know" all the time. It's, you know, annoying.

Don't call the interviewer by his or her first name.

Don't slip into a speech-making or preaching tone of voice. You're not on the Senate floor. You are in a conversation. Make sure you don't bellow.

Don't mumble.

Don't chatter while the interviewer is reviewing your resume. Let him read it in peace.

Don't interpret items on your resume until you are asked. Your resume should be self-explanatory. If additional details are needed, the interviewer will ask for them.

Don't try to overpower the recruiter with bragging or overstatement. He won't respond well, and he is probably skilled in recognizing distortions of background and experience.

Don't lie about anything. Sometimes candidates lie about their salary. Recruiters often ask for proof, such as a W-2 form.

Don't criticize your present employer too much. If it's a bad situation, you can mention it, but don't harp on it. You don't want to be considered a crank.

Don't ever get angry or even irritated during the interview. You can be firm — not angry — if the questioning becomes improper or begins to slip into irrelevant areas.

Don't answer questions that you don't want to answer because you consider them to be too personal — and explain your reasoning.

Don't look at your watch during the interview. This tends to hurry things along. Let the interviewer set the pace.

Don't ask, "Will I get the job?" or, "Can I have the job?" These questions tend to box the recruiter in and he won't like that. Rather say, "I hope you can consider me as a candidate for this job," or "I'm really interested in this job."

Don't talk about salary until later in the hiring process or until the interviewer brings it up.

Dos

Do make sure your hands are attractive. This means spotlessly clean with trimmed nails.

Do make sure that your hair is in place and conservative.

Do pay attention to your scent. Women with powerful perfumes and men with intense colognes can destroy interviews. Again, moderation is recommended.

Do go to the bathroom before you visit the employment lobby. It is embarrassing to interrupt an interview to "go," and you want to be as comfortable as possible during this "pressure cooker" happening.

Do get a good night's sleep before each day that you search for employment. If you yawn in the lobby or smother a yawn during the interview, it will cost you. Be rested and at your alert best.

Do look the interviewer in the eye. Recruiters place a lot of emphasis on eye contact.

Do try to sparkle. Use gestures in your conversation. Make sure they are smooth and emphatic.

Do smile.

Do make sure you get the interviewer's name right and use it a few times during the interview.

Do have some money with you. You never know what might happen. The interviewer might tell you he'd like you to take a cab to a consulting psychologist's office. You never want to be in the embarrassing position of having to say, "I don't have any money with me." The employer will almost always pay any expenses for something the company asks you to do.

Do scout the place of employment before your interview if you can. If you plan on applying at a bank, walk through the public areas a day or two before your interview. You can get an excellent idea about dress modes and the working atmosphere by observing for a few minutes. Even if you adjust your approach or appearance because of your observation, stay on the conservative side.

Do take notes if you wish. After all, the interviewer takes them. Why shouldn't you? You might consider writing down some questions before you go into the interview. A few good questions (and ones you should want the answers to) are:

- Is it your policy to promote from within, or are a lot of senior jobs filled by experienced people from the outside?
- Is there a union that I will be asked or perhaps required to join? What union is it? What are the initiation dues and the monthly dues?
- Are there training programs available to me so that I might learn and grow?
- How often is job performance reviewed?

Do let the interviewer set the pace of the interview. Let him lead with the questions.

Do let the interviewer decide when the interview is over.

Do ask the interviewer when you will hear from him again.

What You Will Be Asked

The 1975 edition of *The Endicott Report* of Northwestern University lists 50 questions frequently asked by employers in interviews with college seniors. You should spend a lot of time considering these questions and practicing answers to them.

1. What are your long-range and short-range goals and objectives; when and why did you establish these goals; and how are you preparing yourself to achieve them?

2. What specific goals, other than those related to your occupation, have you established for yourself in the next 10 years?

3. What do you see yourself doing five years from now?

4. What do you *really* want to do in life?

5. What are your long-range career objectives?

6. How do you plan to achieve your career goals?

7. What are the most important rewards you expect in your business career?

8. What do you expect to be earning in five years?

9. Why did you choose the career for which you are preparing?

10. Which is more important to you: the money or the type of job?

11. What do you consider to be your greatest strengths and weaknesses?

12. How would you describe yourself?

13. How do you think a friend or professor who knows you well would describe you?

14. What motivates you to put forth your greatest effort?

15. How has your college experience prepared you for your career?

16. Why should I hire you?

17. What qualifications do you have that make you think that you will be successful in your career?

18. How do you determine or evaluate success?

19. What do you think it takes to be successful in a company such as ours?

20. In what ways do you think you can make a contribution to our company?

21. What qualities should a successful manager possess?

22. Describe the relationship that should exist between a supervisor and those reporting to him or her.

23. W" at two or three accomplishments have given you the most satisfaction? Why?

24. Describe your most rewarding college experience.

25. If you were hiring a graduate for this position, what qualities would you look for?

26. Why did you select your college or university?

27. What led you to choose your field of major study?

28. What college subjects did you like best? Why?

29. What college subjects did you like least? Why?

30. If you could do so, how would you plan your academic study differently? Why?

31. What changes would you make in your college or university? Why?

32. Do you have plans for continued study? An advanced degree?

33. Do you think that your grades are a good indication of your academic achievement?

34. What have you learned from participation in extracurricular activities?

35. In what kind of work environment are you most comfortable?

36. How do you work under pressure?

37. In what part-time or summer jobs have you been most interested? Why?

38. How would you describe the ideal job for you following graduation?

39. Why did you decide to seek a position with this company?

40. What do you know about our company?

41. What two or three things are most important to you in your job?

42. Are you seeking employment in a company of a certain size? Why?

43. What criteria are you using to evaluate the company for which you hope to work?

44. Do you have a geographical preference? Why?

45. Will you relocate? Does relocation bother you?

46. Are you willing to travel?

47. Are you willing to spend at least six months as a trainee?

48. Why do you think you might like to live in the community in which our company is located?

49. What major problem have you encountered and how did you deal with it?

50. What have you learned from your mistakes?

Stress Interviews

College students sometimes like to play business games. One fraternity used to have a special ritual for potential pledges. On the night of the interview, potential pledges waited around in rooms at the fraternity house until their turn came. Then, in turn, they were led to the basement, given a lighted candle, and told to knock three times on the door.

A voice from inside boomed, "Who seeks to enter?" The candidate would blurt his name and was told to enter. It was dark in the basement. The candidate was led to one end of the basement from where he could see the 40 or so members of the fraternity.

The candidate was told to hold the candle up high in front of him, to look at the candle, and to tell all about himself. Then the candidate had to deliver a two-minute speech about himself, punctuated by shouts of "louder" and "Keep your eyes on the candle" from the members. At the end of the autobiography, there was a question period. A panel of about three members would question the candidate in imperial voices calculated to intimidate him. "Candidate, just why do you want to pledge this fraternity?" After a few such questions, there would be questioning from the floor. The trouble was that all the questions came at once. "Howoldareyouwhyareyoumajoringin marketingwhatsportsdoyoumanybrothersandsisters whathighschooldid Answer that, candidate!" Finally, after the candidate had made a poor attempt to handle 10 questions at once, somebody would say, "Get him outta here." The guy behind him blew the candle out and led him out of the room.

The candidate was taken to another room, where he would sweat out the result. After all the candidates went through candlelight, the members voted on them. Any candidate could be blackballed in secret ballot. Very few were blackballed, but the potential pledges didn't know that. They sweated it out.

The purpose of that "interview" was nothing more than harassment. Business uses a similar technique for quite different reasons. The technique is called the stress interview. And that is just what it sounds like. They put the screws to you. The interviewer's mood or tone of voice might be tough or hostile. Or you might be asked extremely personal questions.

Stress interviews are usually used with candidates for high-level jobs. But college recruiters sometimes use them, too, and recruiters interviewing candidates for sales jobs use them to see if the candidate is easily intimidated.

If you find yourself in a stress interview, it will probably mean the recruiter is trying to find out one of two things:

• How far you can be pushed before you dig in. What is your reaction to browbeating? Do you get angry or do you get judiciously firm?

Don't get visibly angry. It is a plus for you to become brusque and inflexible, for employers aren't impressed by timid people. But don't blow up.

• What your rattle quotient is. If you go to pieces under pressure, the recruiter probably won't want to gamble on you.

Sometimes the questioning gets into areas where an employment interview has no business going. Candidates will answer questions that they know are improper. They answer because they are afraid to shut the recruiter off, and the pressure soars.

Sometimes a recruiter will ask a question such as, "Have you had an extramarital affair in the last five years?" If you simply answer "Yes," or "No," you come off as wishy-washy. You should let the recruiter know that he has exceeded the mark. Your answer should be something like, "I have no idea what that could possibly have to do with my ability to do this job." You probably shouldn't say, "I refuse to answer that question." There's no need to be extremely blunt when you can be diplomatically blunt.

If the recruiter still presses, you can insist, saying something like, "I'll just pass that question." Maybe you want to answer the question. Even so, you should let the recruiter know that you don't think he should be asking it. You can say something like, "I don't think that has anything to do with my value as an employee, but the answer is 'no'."

Women are often asked impertinent questions. A recruiter might say, "I see you've been married six months. Do you plan to have children?" and you might say, "Not immediately." The recruiter, concerned that you might be using rhythm, might then ask, "What form of birth control do you practice?" Shut him off. Say something like, "Oh, I don't want to go into that." If you want to talk about it, throw him a jab anyway. Tell him, "First of all, that's an illegal question. Secondly, it doesn't have a thing to do with how well I can perform my job. But I will tell you that I'm on the pill." If you do that, you have alerted the recruiter that you aren't going to be bullied, yet you have given him the answer he wanted to hear. A double play.

Remember that you have just as much right to set the outer limits of the interview as the recruiter does.

Silence is another pressure tactic a recruiter can use to test the poise of the candidate. A recruiter might ask you, "What are your professional goals?" And you start talking. The interviewer starts to write, breaking off the eye contact. You talk for a minute or so and run out of things to say. He keeps on writing. Silence. Pressure starts to build. Another 20 seconds of silence. The pressure is almost unbearable. He writes some more and maybe glances at you once or twice. At this point, the unskillful candidate will start to babble. If the candidate keeps his silence, a minute or two will pass before the recruiter says, "Is that all?" Unskillful candidates will babble at this point, too.

What you should do is take control of the situation. After the silence has become apparent, and as soon as the pressure starts to mount, you should ask a question: "Is that the sort of information you were interested in?" or "Did I go into enough detail to give you a clear idea of my goals?" That puts the ball back in the recruiter's court. It forces him to break his silence, and it takes the pressure off.

Committee Interviews

Some organizations, including many government agencies and federally funded social action groups, require job applicants to interview in front of a committee of seven or eight people.

Committee interviews are not engineered to be stress interviews, but that is what they turn out to be. They are tough, pressure-packed situations. Some candidates find the idea of going up against a gang of interviewers shattering, and they fall apart.

Invariably there is one individual who sits there and doesn't say a thing. He doesn't even look at you. He is extremely unnerving. You wonder what he is thinking about. He probably isn't thinking about anything. Forget about him.

One reason committee interviews are so tough is that while you are answering one person's questions, the other seven people are framing their questions. So you have a string of stiff questions coming at you. Don't get rattled. Don't blurt out the first thing that comes to mind. If somebody asks you a long, complex question that requires a thoughtful answer, a good tactic is to say, "I'm going to run it back at you in my own words to make sure I understand it." Then rephrase the question in your own words. That not only removes the possibility of your really misunderstanding the question and blundering into an irrelevant answer, it also gives you time to think. Politicians do that all the time.

Skeletons

There are leaks in almost everyone's program. In job interviewing, the best thing to do is to be totally open and honest about major personal problems and to present your case in the most positive manner. Following are some common problems:

• You've been fired. That's not the tragedy you think it is. Many people have been fired, including me. Some organizations are so famous for firing that if you last more than three or four years, you probably don't have any character. Present the circumstances surrounding your firing completely and with little or no interpretive comment. Wait for questions. You couldn't get along with your boss? So what. It happens all the time. Inadequate on the job? If you were recently promoted, you obviously bit off more than you could chew comfortably. If you have been on the job for several years, perhaps management changed your job content, or somebody wanted you out and set you up, or you got stale.

• You're a college senior or a new graduate with a low grade point. Tell the recruiter why. Did you have extracurricular activities — sports, a job, campus politics? Maybe you had difficulty in certain kinds of required subjects, such as courses involving math. If you have a low grade point and no activities, you have a problem that you had better think about and design a positive presentation. Otherwise, you're in trouble.

• You have bad credit or recently declared bankruptcy. Again, lay it out. Hiding the facts won't make them go away. Why are you having financial difficulty? If you tell the employer the reasons, there will be those who will turn you down, but the employer who hires you has obviously extended you conditional forgiveness. And you won't have to work with the constant fear of having to explain your troubles at a later and perhaps embarrassing time. Employers frequently run credit checks for some jobs.

• You have a record of job-hopping. Why? Money? Climate? Lack of growth opportunity? If you left three jobs in two years, and you left all three because you couldn't get along with the boss, you have troubles. Think of all the factors that caused you to leave each job, and again present your case in the most positive manner.

• Your career is lagging. You have been out of college for five years and your salary is only equal to what brand new graduates are paid. Many potential employers would wonder about you because your lack of financial growth could indicate that you aren't very good. Again, present your case in the most positive manner: poor company profitability and the fact that no one has grown much recently could be a good reason. Or maybe you turned down a promotion and/or transfer because of job interest, geographic preference, or family responsibilities, and your refusal held you back. A logical and sensible and *honest* presentation can be put together with a little thought and a little rehearsal.

• You are a felon. One candidate I interviewed impressed me with his directness. He told me at the start of the interview that he had just been paroled from a state prison after serving three years of a five-year sentence for bankrobbery. He told me he learned welding in prison and wanted a welding job. His presentation was flawless. He told me everything and let me make my own decision. Hiding a background like his would have been impossible, so he didn't try. If his past had been discovered at a later date, it would have destroyed any job security he might have had. I made him an offer, which he turned down in favor of a better one somewhere else. If you have been convicted of a felony, don't try to hide it.

• You are an alcoholic. Tell the recruiter about it. Any job offer probably will include a written statement that you will keep your job only by staying on the wagon. Excessive absenteeism or any drinking will mean the end. That is the way it is, and I would think this would be all a controlled alcoholic would need. Employers don't offer jobs to active alcoholics.

• Your health is bad. Spill everything. Hide nothing. If you start a job and then have to leave it soon because of health or, worse yet, get fired because of poor attendance, the next job will be that much tougher to find. If you and your new employer have a complete understanding, he will be inclined to be lenient if health becomes a problem after you go to work.

• You are divorced. Lay it out. Perhaps you have dependent children or alimony to pay. Divorce is not uncommon. It is certainly not something to be ashamed of or to hide. Let the recruiter know what your circumstances are.

• There is a gap in your employment record. Where were you? Traveling? Unemployed? In jail? In the hospital? Let the employer know.

Recruiters have an uncanny ability to sense something fishy. If a recruiter is interested in you but is in any way suspicious, he will check your background very thoroughly before making an offer. If he discovers a skeleton in your closet that you didn't tell him about—no offer. If he hires you without the thorough check and discovers the skeleton later, you could get fired. At best, your career in that organization would be dead because your employer couldn't trust you. If you tell the potential employer everything in an honest and positive way and he then makes you an offer, you are golden. No skeletons, no ghosts, and you have received a magnificent vote of confidence from your new employer. It might not be easy, and you might be turned down many times, but the alternatives should not be acceptable to you.

Item G

What You Owe The Interviewer

In any job interview, you owe the interviewer four things. If you don't deliver them, the employer might not deliver an offer. You owe the interviewer:

• A professional attitude and appearance.

• An indication that you know something about the company.

• A clear idea of what you want to do.

• A sales pitch.

Those four points are what the next four chapters are about.

PROFESSIONALISM
Look and act like you have the job

Students sometimes ask me, "Why did I go to college? Why didn't I go to charm school?" The fact is that job candidates who combine a college education with social grace have a lot going for them.

Employers want professionals. The most meaningful definition of a professional is one who takes his or her work seriously, is deeply committed to doing a good job, and is concerned about the ethical standards and the level of quality of the industry or profession. But the hiring process is largely superficial. It is hard for employers to determine which job candidates are true professionals and which are not.

Therefore, as far as job hunting goes, "be a professional" translates to "look and act like people who work in the field you're interviewing for."

Most experienced people in any field know this. Many entry level people either don't know it or ignore it. College men show up for job interviews wearing sneakers, fraternity T-shirts, and/or letter sweaters. They look as if they are going to a beer party rather than to a job interview. College women sometimes show up braless, wearing sandals, and occasionally blue jeans. They don't get hired.

In almost any professional hiring situation, when two candidates have equal credentials, the one who is more in the Dale Carnegie-*Gentleman's Quarterly-Harper's*

Bazaar-Corporate Boardroom vein will get the job. That is unscientific, unimaginative, and perhaps short-sighted. But that's how it works. Employers judge people largely on appearance and on manners.

Two "war" stories should help drive this point home.

Last year on my campus, an accounting student with a high grade point average interviewed with a recruiter from a public accounting firm. He was a first-rate candidate, and I thought he would be invited in for a second interview. The recruiter passed him up.

"Why?" I asked the recruiter later.

"Because his shirttail was sticking out," the recruiter said.

"You mean you'd pass up a blue-chip candidate like him just because his shirttail was hanging out?" I asked.

"Look," the recruiter said, "I'm interviewing 400 people, and we're going to end up hiring only 5. I don't have to take any chances."

One student interviewing through my placement center was having a terrible time finding a job. For interviews, he had been wearing black shoes, white socks, blue pants that were too short, a cheap sport coat that was too small, a scorched white shirt, and a one-dollar tie.

I asked him if he had $200. He said he did. "Then go to Redwood & Ross," I told him, "and say you want a business suit. If it costs less than $125 (1975 prices), don't buy it. Don't buy a shirt under $10. Get $40 shoes and some long socks. No more cheapo ties. Spend $10 on a tie. And don't have your mother launder your shirts any more."

He went shopping, and when he came in three days later, he looked like a million bucks. And he got a job. Fast.

You may not like the clothing "rules" that are in effect when you apply for a job. You may think they're absurd pronouncements of an overfed generation with twisted values. You may feel that they stifle individualism or freedom of expression.

Perhaps you feel that if you are a morally decent, hard-working, competent person, it shouldn't matter to a potential employer whether you wear Levis or Brooks Brothers. Well, it does matter. "Rules" of dress are "operative," and if you want to succeed in the job market, you have to follow them. You are playing in the employers' sandbox.

When students balk at dressing up for job interviews, I point out to them that recruiters are extremely establishment, highly conservative in their dress. I tell students, "The recruiter looks the way he looks for one of two reasons: his environment forces him to look like that or he likes the way he looks, which means he doesn't like the way you look, which in turn means you aren't going to get the job."

People hire in their own image. The closer you look to the person who is interviewing you, the better your chances are.

Professional dress codes are mostly unwritten. But they exist, and they can be rigid. There are few nonlabor jobs where employers are not concerned to some degree with how employees — and job candidates — are dressed. Even newspaper reporters, who for years looked as if they were outfitted on the Bowery, are starting to dress up. Drop into any big city newsroom, and you will see women in business suits and some men in suits that actually fit — a shocking departure from newspaper tradition.

When I started working at the university, I thought I had arrived at the one type of institution where you could do and wear anything you wanted. Not so.

In my first week on the job, I noticed that other people were wearing sport shirts to work. It was hot and there was no air-conditioning, so one day I wore a nice-looking golf shirt. My boss, a dean who was noted for being liberal, asked me, "Are you on vacation?"

I said, "No, I'm not. But I guess you don't like the sport shirt."

"Right," he said.

"Okay," I said, "but why?"

"You're supposed to be the broker between the business community and the academic community," he said, "and I think you ought to look like a businessman. What's more, some day you're going to be called to a meeting with the Chancellor without any advance notice, and I don't want any of my directors showing up in a sport shirt."

That was the end of my days as a libertine.

How to Dress

When dressing for job interviews, it is almost impossible to be too conservative. Most employers regard conservative dress as a sign of good judgment.

What does conservative dress mean?

For men applying for a professional job:

• A conservative suit and tie. John T. Molloy, clothing expert and author of *Dress for Success*, recommends that if a new college graduate can afford only one suit, it should be a dark blue solid. "If he can afford a second," says Molloy, "it should be a gray pinstripe, preferably with a vest." Molloy recommends solid-colored ties, polka-dotted ties or the "rep" tie (conservative stripes).

• Conservative shoes, preferably with laces.

• Long socks.

• A long-sleeve shirt, preferably a light, solid color.

Men should avoid:

• Anything loud.

• Sports coats.

• Leisure suits.

122

• Short-sleeve shirts. Molloy decrees that you should "never, ever, as long as you live, wear a short sleeve shirt for any business purpose, no matter whether you're the office boy or the president of the company." He says short-sleeve shirts "pack no psychological authority or power."

• Platform shoes. White shoes. Loafers.

• White socks. (Is there anybody left who doesn't know that white socks are taboo?)

• Fuzzy wool socks.

• Bow ties. Molloy says men who wear bow ties aren't taken seriously.

• Flashy watches or other unusual accessories.

• Fraternity pins, rings with fraternity insignia, or other organizational trappings. Except for an occasional Phi Beta Kappa key, recruiters do not display organizational paraphernalia. They don't wear Masonic pins, Elks tooths, Rotary buttons. You should avoid them, too. You never know what might offend someone.

• Too much cologne or after-shave lotion. A little cologne is alright, but if you're going to smell of anything, it's probably best to smell of soap.

For women applying for professional jobs:

• A conservative, well-fitting skirt and jacket with a contrasting blouse underneath is best. Most recruiters say they have no objection to pantsuits, but a few do. And I have never heard a recruiter express a preference for pantsuits. So to maximize your chances, it is only logical for you to wear a skirt and jacket.

• Conservative shoes.

• Pantyhose (natural shade). If you are wearing open-toed or open-heeled shoes, wear pantyhose without reinforced toes or heels.

• Subdued, flattering makeup. (If you don't like makeup, and if you make a good appearance without it, fine.)

Women should avoid:

• Sexy clothes. A woman who advertises her figure in job interviews is encouraging male chauvinism—and probably will get it. If the interviewer is a hard-nosed businessman, he probably will wonder: "Why is she trying to influence me with that approach? Why isn't she trying to impress me with her intelligence?" So don't sex it up. No ultrashort skirts, no supertight sweaters, no deep-cut fronts. Recruiters don't like it.

Said one recruiter: "I have a mixed reaction to the woman who tries to use sex appeal to sway the interviewer—the see-through blouse, the low-cut dress, the short skirt and a lot of leg being shown. One reaction is amusement, the other is pure disgust."

The sexy approach can be particularly devastating when the sexpot shows up for an interview and the recruiter turns out to be a woman. Women who have made it on their brains don't have much respect for women who are trying to make it on their bodies.

• Exotic shoes, sandals.
• High-fashion outfits.
• Loud colors or patterns.
• Heavy makeup or long false eyelashes.
• Heavy perfume.
• Dangling bracelets, prominent earrings or any other wild jewelry.
• Anything faddy, such as rings on eight fingers.
• Obviously all clothing on both men and women should be well pressed and immaculate.

Many people who have a few years' experience and who are very good in their field either ignore or minimize the importance of dressing for job interviews. They think their talent or their credentials will put them over. Often they don't.

NOTE: Dress standards vary from city to city. People in San Francisco dress differently from people in Dallas. What works in Los Angeles might not work in New York. Job candidates should find out what these geographical differences are and dress accordingly.

Dress codes also differ according to the field. Advertising agencies and public relations firms generally don't mind a touch of flamboyance. Public accounting firms and banks want their people to look like registered Republicans. If you walk from New York's Madison Avenue to Wall Street, you can see the difference in the styles. The coloration of the locals changes.

If you are an entry level candidate, you should do some careful scouting of the prevailing dress patterns in whatever field you want to get into.

TIP: The president of the United States usually sets the dress standards for the American businessman. Hat manufacturers are happy when the president starts to wear a hat, because hat sales shoot up. If the president started wearing sport coats to press conferences, sport coats would be "in." If he grew a moustache, you would see a lot more senior businessmen with moustaches. If you are male, you can't go wrong in most businesses if you dress like the president—as long as the president is a man.

The Hair Thing

The arrival of long hair for men in the mid-1960s was a shock to the central nervous system of the American business establishment. Men were not supposed to look like that! Businessmen regarded long hair as seditious, communistic, and a sacrilegious, subversive outrage. They felt it probably should be unconstitutional. The typical businessman scorned any man whose hair was longer than Prince Valiant's as a crackpot, a Bolshevik, or both.

The attitude of business was partly a narrow-minded reaction indicating distorted values and partly common sense. Employers knew that having long-haired men working for them could hurt their image and, consequently, their profits. Companies began firing men with long hair. They found themselves being hauled into court—and losing, but by the end of the 1960s, long hair had gained almost universal acceptance among young people. High school boys in the smallest North Dakota hamlets looked like rock stars. A college man with short hair was an oddity on almost any campus in the country.

The business community grudgingly came to accept it. *To an extent.*

Recruiters now will say, "We've come to live with long hair," or "The hair thing doesn't bother us anymore." Do not believe it. It does bother them. They are uncomfortable about it. No recruiter is going to announce on network television that "We won't hire any man whose hair hits the collar." Discrimination suits would come raining down on him. But you would have to go a long way before you could find a recruiter who would say he *prefers* long hair, or even likes it. Employers do discriminate. Once again, it's their sandbox.

Any young man who wants to maximize his chances in the job market will have a businessman's haircut. And that means short.

The same thing is true for beards and moustaches. There still is an enormous slice of the business community that finds something un-American about beards. Four hundred recruiters interviewed students in my placement center last year. No more than five had a moustache. None had a beard.

Recruiters do not tell people that they are rejecting candidates for long hair or for beards, but they do discriminate against them. Don't give the recruiter a weapon to "de-select" you. If you have a moustache or a beard, shave it off. If you are a man with long hair, cut it.

Would that be selling out, compromising? Perhaps. But it would not be selling out or compromising on any moral or ethical principle. It is a situation in which you can be practical and pragmatic without giving up your decency as a human being. You do not injure anyone, cheat anyone, or hurt anyone's feelings when you shave off a beard. You do not deprive anyone of his rights when you get a businessman's haircut. What you are compromising on is personal taste. You may feel that you are being deprived of your rights, and there is legal precedent to support that feeling. But you should decide whether you want a job or whether you want to squabble about hair. My advice is to yield on hair and, if you are reform minded, take on some of the more substantial evils of the business world.

Furthermore, your compromise of personal taste might only be temporary. After you've been hired and have been on the job for a while, let your hair grow, raise a beard if you want. You might still have a battle on your hands, but you will have had a chance to demonstrate your competence, and you will be fighting as an insider instead of an outsider.

One final, and unfortunate, note on appearance. It is a harsh fact that employers discriminate against people who are physically unattractive. Anyone who is fat or who has acne is at a serious disadvantage in the job market. That fact should give a fat person added incentive to lose weight. Unlike losing weight, ridding yourself of acne is not simply an exercise in willpower. Acne can't be cured, but it can be treated to improve your appearance. The treatments might involve spending a lot of money for a dermatologist.

Bad teeth could also be a minus for you. If your teeth are ugly because of decay, it would be wise to have them repaired, no matter what the cost. If your teeth are healthy but full of gaps and odd shapes, you might consider cosmetic dentistry. Caps and bridges will do a lot of damage to your pocketbook, but they will help you look better.

Do anything you can to improve your looks. Have your hair done by a good stylist. If you have dandruff, consult a dermatologist. Spend some money if you have to. It will pay off.

Style and Manners

Twenty years ago, when I was a green recruiter, I was sent to an Ivy League university to hire several engineers for technical work and several liberal arts students for our corporate management program. Maybe it was my youthful appearance that caused my first candidate to put his feet on my desk during the interview. My age did not affect my power. I turned the kid down on the spot. You would have, too, if you were the recruiter. Maybe the clod would put his feet on the company president's desk during the final interview.

How about the candidate who brought a bag of peanuts into the interview, offered some, and then ate them during the next 10 minutes of conversation about a job he wanted? Or the man who clipped his fingernails during the interview, or the woman who plunked her elbows on the desk and her chin in her hands and stayed that way through a 20-minute conversation?

Don't let anybody cast a negative vote on you because of your manners.

What are the rules? For openers, do not bother to read traditional etiquette books. They are full of absurd pronouncements, based not on logic but on archaic codes rooted in upper-class snobbery. The rules of introduction (who you introduce to whom and why) are a baffling maze. Instead of memorizing all of that claptrap, concentrate on being polite, being warm and friendly, and being graceful with your body.

128

Being warm and friendly means being natural. Relax a bit. A job interview isn't quite as bad as a Marine Corps inspection. You don't have to sit at attention. You don't have to spit sharp "Yes sirs" at the recruiter. You can be conversational; just don't get chummy. And be cheerful. Don't get hostile, belligerent, or abrasive. If you do, you're not going to get hired.

Being polite doesn't mean being archly formal: it means showing respect for the interviewer as a person. Pay attention to what he or she says. Don't interrupt. If you go to a restaurant with the recruiter, don't bully the waitress. Open doors for the people you are with if you are in the logical place to be a door opener. Don't eat like Henry the Eighth. Stay alert. If you're taken into somebody's office, don't sit down unless you're invited to sit. Don't do anything that's obviously boorish.

Being graceful with your body includes sitting in a dignified but comfortable position; using smooth gestures instead of jerky, irritating motions; not sitting down with a thud, not leaning on the interviewer's desk. In other words, not being a lout.

It's all quite simple.

Drinking

Many a sales manager will send any candidate for a sales job out to lunch with the company's champion martini drinker. If the candidate comes back smashed, he doesn't get the job. The sales manager figures that if they can get the guy drunk at lunch while he's a candidate for a job, what the hell is he going to be like after he starts to work, when he's more relaxed, when nobody is scrutinizing him?

If a recruiter or your potential boss takes you out to lunch at some point in the hiring process, don't be afraid to order a drink, but if you are sitting with three managers from the company and you're the only one with a drink, you're in trouble.

If you are the first person at the table the waitress asks about a drink, you should pass. Say something like, "Check one of the others first. I haven't decided." Then if they order a drink and you want one, go ahead.

You should be extremely reluctant to order a second drink. Let the others have a second if they want while you nurse your first drink. If the others encourage you to order a second drink, you can say something like, "No thanks. I have to be extra sharp this afternoon. I'm a candidate for employment."

It's different in the evening. If you are taken out to dinner or to a bar, you probably are safe having more than one drink. But you should be very careful that you are not the most drunk.

KNOWING ABOUT THE COMPANY

Research the organization

"Incidentally, what do you people make?"

That is the most devastating question you can ask a recruiter for a manufacturing company. And although it is incredibly stupid, candidates ask that question frequently.

When I was a recruiter for a manufacturer of large motors, I interviewed hundreds of people for jobs in such fields as accounting, personnel, sales, and data processing. Often an interview would be going along smoothly and then, halfway through, the candidate would hit me with "What do you make?" It always floored me.

Our employment lobby was peppered with company literature. Yet some candidates who didn't know anything at all about the company would spend 15 minutes waiting for an interview reading *Sports Illustrated*, *McCall's*, or *Field and Stream*.

My office was right next to the manufacturing area. Just outside my door, a huge press punching out laminations was going kachunga-kachunga. Through a window in my office the candidate could see golden weld flashes. If he came through the plant to get to my office, as some candidates did, he could see blue curls of steel from milling machines and shavers all over the place. Obviously, it wasn't a dairy, but whenever a candidate asked what we made, I always had a sadistic urge to answer, "Ice cream," and follow that up with, "Figure that out, imbecile."

I never said that, but usually I would say something sarcastic, such as, "It's a shame that most people don't recognize that we're the third largest manufacturer of motors in the United States. We make equipment up to 5,000 horsepower, BIG stuff, and it's too bad that more people don't know about that."

In response, many candidates would say, "Yeah, it is a shame that more people don't know about that." The dummies didn't even know that I was castigating them. Others would say, "I guess I should have known that before I came to talk to you." Anyone who said that was starting to bail himself out. We might eventually get along. But he had severely hurt his chances by not knowing what our company did for a living.

For almost any job, the recruiter is likely to ask you, "How do you feel about our company?" or "What do you know about us?" If you have done your homework, you can say, "I'm very interested in going to work in quality control for your company because of its products (and you can elaborate), because of the market you serve (elaborate), and because of your solid reputation and history (elaborate)."

If you can give such an answer, you're hitting home.

But if your answer is, "I don't know much about the company," or "Nothing," you've committed a serious blunder and you probably won't be able to recover. Your interview will probably be over, even though it may take about five minutes to wind down.

The candidate who doesn't know anything about the company is merely responding to the words on the front door saying "Employment Office." If Company A makes him a job offer, he will probably accept. If it doesn't, he will go to the next door that says "Employment Office," and if they make him an offer, he will probably accept that. But those companies probably won't make offers to the candidate who doesn't know — and consequently doesn't seem to care — about them.

The recruiter, in most cases, comes into the interview prepared. He has, at some point, spent some time preparing for the interviews for the job you are applying for. He may have spent an hour with the department manager to find out what special specifications the manager has in mind. Assuming that the recruiter has prepared for the interview, you are a fool if you don't prepare, too.

Candidate ignorance of the company is a common complaint of recruiters. Many consider it an outrage. Many recruiters say they don't expect applicants to know a lot about their company, just the basics.

But when you are looking for a job, you should, whenever possible, exceed the minimum expectations. Anybody can do the minimum. You want to be as strong a candidate as possible, and anything you do that shows initiative and shows that you are alert, aware, and interested in the company will increase your chances. It can be the difference between being hired and not being hired, particularly in a tight job market or any other time when there is a lot of competition for jobs. So you should find out as much about the company as you can.

Said the recruiter for one company, "I won't take away from the person if he doesn't know a lot about the company, but I'll view it as a bonus if he does. We're not a public corporation, so it takes a little digging. I asked one applicant what he knew about the company, and he gave me the whole life history of the company. That has to be impressive. I'm not saying that person was hired only because he knew about the company, but it shows good overall interest in the company."

Where to Find Out

In most cases, the company literature will tell you most of what you should know. One of the reasons companies put together pamphlets and brochures is to inform prospective employees about the organization's products, services, and employee benefits. Any company whose stock is publicly held publishes an annual report. An annual report is a public relations tool, and most contain not only financial information but also information on new plants and new products.

Company literature is easy to get. One way is to phone or write to the company personnel office before your interview and ask them to send you the literature. High school guidance offices, college placement centers, and chambers of commerce usually have ample information about any major employer in their area.

> **TIP:** A slick trick is to openly carry the company literature into the interview with you. The recruiter will like that. You're carrying his flag. There's a strong chance that he had a major role in the writing of the literature, so if you tell him, "I read this stuff with great interest," you're saying you read *his* stuff with great interest.
>
> At some point in the interview, you might want to say, "There's something here on page 6 that I have a couple of questions about." Then you turn to page 6 and have the material underlined.
>
> The recruiter will probably know that you're greasing him up, but he'll like it anyway.

To go beyond the minimum and get in-depth information about a company, you might have to do some creative digging. If you know a reliable person who works for

134

the company, you have an excellent primary source. If not, the public library is a good place to start.

If you are interested in a large, nationwide company, there probably will have been magazine articles about it in the last year. You can find them by looking up the company in the *Readers' Guide to Periodical Literature*, which will be in the library. Your library also will probably have an index of *New York Times* stories and copies of the papers. The library in whatever city the company is headquartered might have a history of the company. Ask your librarian for further suggestions.

Most large and medium-sized companies have employee magazines that are produced once a month or so by their public relations department or by an outside public relations agency. The purpose of these "house organs" is to maintain the morale of employees by keeping them informed of company developments and employee policies. (The purpose of some employee publications, however, is to cram management propaganda down employees' throats.)

Some employee publications concentrate on such things as company picnics and the company bowling team. They won't be very helpful. Others contain information about new products, new departments, new plants, and new projects. They sometimes have features about executives or about sales, manufacturing, or management techniques — from your standpoint, very helpful. That sort of information can give you insight into company priorities. Many employee publications carry in every issue a column by the company president or chairman of the board. Some presidents' messages are pure blather, but others have some substance and can give you some idea of the prevailing management philosophy in the company.

If you have a friend working for the company, ask him if he has any recent employee publications. If you don't know anyone at the company, you can phone or write to the company's public relations department and ask if they will send you some recent issues. Or you can phone the public relations department and ask if you can go in and read some of the recent issues in the office.

What You Should Know

Here are some examples of different types of organizations and some basic information you should have about them. This is not a comprehensive list, but it should give you a general idea of what information you should know about any employer.

For a Job with a Manufacturing Company

(for any office job or factory supervisory job)

• What products does the company make? Be particularly observant for secondary product lines. This information is usually in the annual report or other corporate literature.
• What is the company's financial status?
• What has the company's stock been doing?
• What is the company's growth record?
• Where are the company's plants?
• What is the company's position in the industry?
• What is the major competition?

For a Job as a Teacher, School Administrator or Staff Specialist

• How many schools in the district?
• What is the bargaining agent (if there is one) for teachers, administrators, and specialists?
• What is the socioeconomic makeup of the district?
• If it is a parochial school, who operates it?

For an Insurance Company Job

- What kind of insurance does the company sell?
- Is it national or regional?
- How does the company stand in the industry?

For a Job in a Department Store

- Is the store locally owned or is it part of a national chain?
- How many stores does the company have at shopping centers in the area?
- What is the store's financial picture?
- What are the store's major competitors?

For a Social Service Agency

- What are the objectives of the agency?
- Where does it get its funding?
- What are some of its programs?

For a Job with an Airline

- What areas does the airline serve?
- Where is its corporate headquarters?
- What is the financial record of the airline?
- What is its position in the industry?

For a Hospital Job

- Who operates the hospital? Is it a private corporation, governmental unit, a religious order?
- Does it have any specialties, such as cardiology or obstetrics?

For a Job at a Newspaper

- Is it a morning or afternoon paper?
- Does the company publish two papers, one in the morning and one in the afternoon?
- Does the paper own a radio or television station?
- What is the competition?
- What is the paper's circulation?

• Has the paper been gaining or losing circulation?
• Has the paper been making or losing money?
• How wide a geographical area does the paper serve?

For a Hotel Job

• How many rooms does the hotel have?
• Is the hotel part of a chain?
• Has it been making or losing money?
• How old is the hotel?
• Has it changed hands recently?
• What is the major competition?

For a Job in a Bank

• Are there any branches?
• How does the bank compare in size with other banks in town?
• Is it a national- or state-chartered bank?

Get the drift?

10

SAY WHAT YOU WANT TO DO

Hire the recruiter to help you find a job

A few years ago a likable young man with a towering grade point in electrical engineering was about to graduate on my campus. A prestigious corporation was interested in talking to him because there aren't many candidates with such a high grade point in electrical engineering.

The interview lasted 10 minutes.

The recruiter, one of the best on the circuit, told me later, "You'd better straighten that kid out because he's not going to get a job."

That startled me because he was an exceptional candidate, and I thought he would have companies eating out of his hand.

The recruiter told me what had happened in the interview. It seems the conversation went like this:

> **Recruiter:** What would you like to do?
>
> **Candidate:** Oh, I'm interested in a lot of things.
>
> **Recruiter:** Are you interested in going into our design operation?
>
> **Candidate:** Yes, that sounds good.
>
> **Recruiter:** What about our development program?

Candidate: Yes, I think I'd like that.

Recruiter: How would you feel about a job in sales?

Candidate: Sure.

Recruiter: What about working in application?

Candidate: I'd like that fine.

Then the recruiter asked him where he'd like to work. "Anywhere but Milwaukee," was the reply. "It's too cold."

Recruiter: How about Los Angeles?

Candidate: No, that's too big.

Recruiter: Well, we have some labs in New Mexico.

Candidate: Too hot.

Recruiter: We have a development in Connecticut.

Candidate: I don't like the East Coast.

The recruiter had thrown four jobs at the candidate, and he had said yes to every one. The recruiter tried three different locations, and he said no to all three. Here is someone who will do anything, and he won't go anywhere to do it. The question is, Where does the recruiter go next with the candidate? With whom does he set up the next interview?

The recruiter told the young man, in effect, "Thank you very much. I've enjoyed talking to you. And don't let the door hit you as you leave." It was all over.

There are two major points to be learned from that young man's experience:

• When you go into a job interview, you should have a pretty good idea of what you want to do.

• You have to be at least open to the idea of going almost anywhere to do it.

Don't Keep the Recruiter Guessing

Unless you are answering a newspaper ad or following a lead for a specific job, you have to give that recruiter some direction. He certainly doesn't know what you want to do. Recruiters don't like candidates who say, "What have you got?" You have to tell them what you want. You don't have to have it narrowed down to the nub: "I want to be the third assistant in the quality control department." But you should be able to give the recruiter some solid idea of what kind of job you hope to get.

• "I want to be an advertising copywriter."
• "I'm interested in selling steel."
• "I'd like to be a buyer for your store, and I'm particularly interested in women's sportswear."

In each of these examples, the recruiter knows exactly where the next interview will be: with the advertising manager, with the sales manager, with the divisional merchandise manager. Then he can start wearing the hat of a particular department manager, and he can screen according to that department head's specifications.

Investigate the corporate setup beforehand. Then, in the interview, you can throw the recruiter two choices. "I'd like to be a buyer for your store. I'm most interested in women's sportswear or carpeting." I wouldn't throw the recruiter three choices because it might appear to be too indiscriminate. If there is going to be a third throw, let the recruiter make it. He might say, "We don't have an opening in women's sportswear or carpeting, but there is a job for an assistant buyer in linens." Are you interested in that?" And you probably are.

If he comes back at you too many times, he might be testing you. So be careful. If the recruiter throws six or seven types of work at you and you are interested in all of them, you risk the fate of the young man who said yes to all four things the recruiter mentioned. The recruiter might start to think you're kind of drifty. If he does suggest a type of work that you're not interested in, tell him you're not interested. If he says, "What about our hardware department?" you can say, "No, I'm not mechanically inclined. I never was interested in fixing things around the house or working with tools and I don't think I'd be comfortable buying hardware."

If you are so anxious to get a job as a department store buyer that you would buy anything, don't just flatly agree to everything the recruiter suggests. If the recruiter mentions four different jobs, explain your position — and qualify it. You can say, "Mr. Recruiter, I want very much to be a buyer for your store. My interests are not narrow, so I would feel comfortable as a buyer in almost any department. I definitely prefer clothing or furniture. But I would be interested in exploring any other areas where there might be an opening." That way you have told the recruiter what you want, but you haven't talked yourself out of a job that might be open.

Usually the recruiter will not give you much help in determining where you would best fit into the organization. When he recommends you for a job you have expressed interest in, he is already gambling on you. If you turn out to be incompetent, the recruiter is in trouble. If the recruiter recommends you for a job in an area *he* has suggested for you, he doubles his jeopardy: not only might you prove incompetent, but you also might hate the job. Then you would go back at him and say, "Mr. Recruiter, I don't like the job you picked out for me." That puts the recruiter on shaky ground. The company has an unhappy employee in an area the recruiter suggested.

There are exceptions. You may want a job driving a lift truck in a factory and the only thing they have open is in "dip and bake." The recruiter will offer you the dip and bake job, and if you take it, you go to work putting electronic parts in goopy stuff and shoving them in an oven. It's a rotten job, and after a couple of weeks you might go in to the recruiter and say, "I don't like it." That recruiter is on solid ground; that was the only way he could hire you. So he can say, "I don't blame you, but that's where everybody starts, and you're going to have to wait until there's an opening somewhere else in the plant and then bid into it."

If you're ambitious and have long-range goals, it can help to tell the recruiter about them. But don't be too specific. If the recruiter asks you, "What do you hope to be doing five years from now?" your answer should be broad, something like: "I hope that in five years I will have had at least two promotions, that I will be responsible for supervising some people and that I would have some budget responsibilities. Beyond that, I hope I have a solid reputation in the company and in the industry. I hope that people seek my advice and that I have some impact on the direction of my area of expertise."

If you say that, you really aren't saying much, except that you want promotions, that you want to manage, that you want to grow, and that you want to have some impact. You haven't committed yourself to a precise job. Almost any recruiter would respond well to an answer like that.

If you are applying for factory work and eventually would like to become a foreman, say so on your application and mention it to the recruiter. Tell him, "I'm very interested in going to work in your factory. I'd like to move through the various jobs until I get into one that has a pretty high degree of skill and eventually I'd like to be a foreman." Employers like production workers who are motivated and who would like to be foremen.

TIP: If you're applying for work in a factory or in any other area where unions and management are constantly squaring off, you can severely hurt your chances by giving some indication that you're a union activist. When I was in high school, I was a union steward. After my freshman year of college, I came back to my home town to look around for a summer job but wasn't getting anywhere. Finally a friend of mine who was in personnel reviewed my resume and said, "You dummy! You said on your resume that you were a union steward. There isn't an employer in town that's going to touch you." So I took it off, and I found someone to hire me.

If you're not interested in management but take pride in being a competent specialist, you can impress the recruiter by saying, "I want to be a technical contributor. I'm not interested in management. I don't want to get into the business of evaluating other people, giving orders, being responsible for the mistakes of others. I am a good engineer (or mathematician, or copywriter, or computer programmer, or draftsman, or machinist, or whatever) and that's what I want to do. Just keep giving me interesting things to do and I'll do them well." Recruiters are always interested in quality, and they will respond well if you get across the idea that you take pride in your work and feel strongly about quality for quality's sake.

Geography

Job applicants do unbelievable things. One woman, a graduating senior, filled in the "Location Preferred" blank on an application with "Work must be on Number 74 bus line." That was the bus line that passed her house. Fat chance.

One young man looking for entry level work said on applications that he wanted to work in quality assurance, which is a small, esoteric part of quality control. What's more, he insisted that the job be in one particular city of 80,000 people. Quality assurance usually involves things like aircraft production and highly technical government contracts. There probably isn't one quality assurance job in that city.

The young man interviewed with several big companies that didn't even have a plant in that city, let alone a quality assurance program. Because of the job and geographical restrictions he listed, the young man went the entire semester without getting a job.

By the end of the school year, enough recruiters had told him he was on the wrong track that he got the message. Desperate, he told me, "I'll go anywhere and do anything for anybody." I knew of a sales opening with a large manufacturing company. I told him about it and he said, "Yeah, I'd like to talk about that." He went for an interview and got the job.

Although the applications say "Location Preferred," recruiters read that as "Location Demanded." Unless you're absolutely locked into a town because of your spouse's job, perhaps, or an elderly and ailing parent, you should keep yourself wide open on geography, at least on the application. If you live in Seattle and you list Seattle as the location preferred, recruiters for national organizations translate that to "This applicant won't move."

So where it says "Location Preferred," put "none" or "anywhere."

What if you're interviewing with a national corporation for a job that you know would be at the company's local facility? No difference. Unless you're *absolutely* locked into your town, put "no preference" for geography. If you don't, you might put yourself out of the running for the job. The recruiter knows that in a few years the company might want to move you to company headquarters in Minneapolis or Houston. And he has to have someone who is flexible.

If a company offers you a job in Yellowknife, in the Northwest Territories, and you hate cold weather, you can always turn it down.

The ideal combination, of course, is a job you like in a city you like. But when jobs are tight in your field, geography should be the first preference to give ground on. Perhaps you want to teach and you don't want to live in Gary, Indiana, or Elizabeth, New Jersey. But if you're really serious about a teaching career and can get an offer only from Gary or Elizabeth, it is better to teach and live there for a couple of years than to sell encyclopedias in some city you like. You can always move on. (Many people discover that paradise isn't all it's cracked up to be when they have a boring job — or have none at all.)

If your career is a major priority in your life, you should follow the sun when you're in your twenties and thirties. Go where the opportunities are best.

11

GIVE A PITCH

Sell the recruiter on why you want the job

Pride in an institution is a personal and emotional thing. For the job candidate, it's a highly exploitable thing.

Consider the loyal alumni who boost the football team. Every university has them, men in their forties and fifties who *really care* whether their alma mater wins or loses. They somehow feel that the performance of a bunch of jocks doing undergraduate work at their university reflects either positively or negatively on them. If the team is having a bad year, the loyal alumnus will grouse about the coach and sheepishly wait until next year. But if the team is stomping on stiff competition, sporting a couple of flashy all-Americans, and ranked among the top ten in the nation, it goes to the head of the Old Grad like a big bite of horseradish. Every day when he picks up his newspaper, he turns right to the sports pages to see what they're writing about next Saturday's game. He constantly lionizes the team to nonbelievers: "Didjya see where Grunch rushed for 187 yards against Nebraska? He's only a sophomore — the next O.J. Simpson for sure." If you want to make Old Grad feel good, praise his team, tell him it's the class of the conference. That will get him puffed up every time.

Recruiters and other executives harbor similar pride about their organizations. They're not as rah-rah about it as Old Grad is about the football team, and their pride has more logic behind it: they are *on* the team, not merely spectators, so their organization's performance really does reflect on them.

Most people care whether the organization they work for is good. And they care what people think about it.

If a recruiter thinks he represents a high-quality company, he is going to be hostile to any job candidate's criticism of the company, unimpressed by indifference to it, and vulnerable to praise of it.

Consider these three statements by candidates to recruiters:

One: I don't think very much of your company, but I've gotta find a job somewhere.

Two: Your company's okay. I'm glad it's in San Diego, because that's where I want to work.

Three: I've done a lot of checking into your company. Everything I've heard convinces me that it's the kind of organization I want to work for.

Very few candidates are dumb enough to make a statement like number one to a recruiter. Some people will say something like number two, but not very many. That's not surprising. What is surprising is that too few applicants say something like statement number three.

The question is, If job candidates are smart enough to know that statements one and two will alienate the recruiter, why don't they follow through to the conclusion that the opposite approach — statement number three — will impress the recruiter?

The hiring process is like sex. If you know that someone of the opposite sex is attracted to you, you probably are flattered and have a warm feeling about that person. A similar relationship is at work in the job interview.

The recruiter is going to assume that his organization is probably the third, fourth, or fourteenth company you've talked to about a job in two weeks. He half expects that you don't much care about his company, that all you're interested in is getting on somebody's payroll. It is your responsibility, at some point in the interview, to correct that impression. *You have to give the recruiter a sales pitch.*

You have to convince the recruiter of two things:

• That you're interested in working for his organization (that is where the recruiter's pride in his organization comes in).

• That you are good.

To convince the recruiter that you want to work for his company, you have to tell him, in effect, that "Your company is kind of special to me. That's the reason I'm talking to you — I really want to work here." And you should give him some reasons.

Doesn't the recruiter know that to a certain extent he's being manipulated? Sure he does. But he responds to it anyway. He likes to be stroked.

> **TIP:** If you don't like the company, don't say that you like it; if you're not impressed by it, don't say you're impressed. You don't have to lie to get a job. Go where you can say it and mean it.

Throughout the interview, you should indicate your interest in the company. But, in addition, you should make your sales pitch in a special speech, and you might want to rehearse it ahead of time.

Flattery isn't the only reason you should give your sales pitch. There is another basic, and perhaps more important, reason. Employers like enthusiasm. It is a truism that enthusiastic people make good employees and unenthusiastic people don't. If you had to choose between two job candidates of about equal qualifications, one who showed a lot of interest in what your organization was doing and one who did not, which would you hire? It probably wouldn't be a difficult choice.

What can happen if you don't show any interest in working for the employer who is interviewing you?

A couple years ago, a young man with good grades in electrical engineering was about to graduate from the university where I work. He took 13 interviews through the campus placement center, and 5 of those companies invited him back for second interviews. But he didn't get one job offer. Five second interviews without a job offer is rare.

The young man was getting panicky, and he came in to talk to me about his lack of success. While he was sitting there, I phoned two executives he had interviewed with to find out what the problem was. They told me they liked the young man but that he hadn't shown any true interest in their companies. So they turned him down. I told the young man what the executives said, and he said he couldn't understand how they were getting that impression.

I knew of a company in town that still had some openings for entry level engineers, so I called the director of engineering at that company. He said, "Send him down. I'd like to talk to him."

I called the engineering director later in the day to find out how the interview went. The director told me he liked the young man but wasn't going to hire him because he hadn't shown any interest in the company. *The young man still hadn't gotten the message!*

I then called the young man and asked *him* how the interview had gone. He said, "Mr.

Stanat, I can't thank you enough for sending me on that interview. That's the most exciting place I've been to. I really want that job."

When I told him they weren't planning to make an offer, he sounded as if he was going to cry. Then I told him it was the same old problem — they didn't think he was interested in them. Then I told him he should call the director back and express some interest in the company and the job. I dictated a statement that he should make to the director.

Fifteen minutes later the director called me, shattering my eardrums with laughter. The young man had just read to him over the phone, without inflection, the statement I had dictated. The director figured out what was going on, and he asked the young man, "Did Stanat tell you to say that?" The young man said, "Yes." But then the director dug a little deeper. He asked the young man, "Are you really serious about what it says in that little speech, or are you just saying it because Stanat told you to?" Then, for the first time, the young man opened up and told an employer how he felt. He said, "I really want to work for you. My conversation with you was the most exciting interview I've had. What can I do to straighten things out?"

The director made him an offer over the phone, and the young man started to work there the next Monday.

Here's another story that illustrates the power of "the pitch."

A division of one of the big three automakers ran a newspaper ad for a sales representative

— someone who would sell cars to dealers — in a large Midwestern city. They got a call from a man in a city 200 miles away who said he would like to interview for the job.

He said, "I can come up at my own expense any time. Matter of fact, today's fine." Real eager.

The recruiter told him to come in the next morning.

The candidate, a good-looking, well-dressed guy, showed up for the interview and gave plenty of indications that he had researched the company. He knew where they were in total car sales, was thoroughly familiar with model terminology, and knew details about the various models.

Throughout the interview, he was constantly saying such things as, "This looks like a really good place to work," and "This is what I've been looking for."

As he left the interview with the recruiter, en route to an interview with a second executive, he stopped off at the secretary's desk and said, "This looks like an excellent place to work. Am I right?" He was really heaping it on. All the executives heard about his comment to the secretary. They were impressed, so they hired him.

In his first week on the job, he used his company credit card to get several of his friends' cars filled with gas, and over the weekend he smashed up the company car. On Monday he was fired. In short, he was one of the worst employees they had ever had. *But he was one of the best candidates.* While he couldn't keep a job, he was a pro at getting one.

152

Techniques

If you know someone who works for the company you are interviewing with and if he or she has told you good things about the company, you have a marvelous device for giving your pitch. You can say to the screener (for a bank), "I know Nancy Jones in your mortgage division. She has a lot of good things to say about how this bank operates and about its general business philosophy. I have enormous respect for Nancy, and her enthusiasm aroused my interest. I checked further and everything I learned verified what she said." You not only make points for yourself, but also for Nancy.

When you pitch the recruiter, don't be satisfied with simply saying, "I really want the job. I very much want to work for this company." Elaborate on that. Tell the recruiter why. And when you do elaborate, the more you know about the company, the better your pitch will be.

If you're applying for a creative job with an advertising agency, find out what ads they've placed, so you can tell the recruiter, "Your ads are refreshing. The Glutz Beer ad shows me that your agency is willing to try a unique approach. The copy in the Pound-Key Typewriter ad was strong, clear, and fresh. I want to work with people who turn out ads like that." (Or if you're applying for an account representative's job, say, "I would be proud and confident selling the work of such a professional creative staff.") Again — if you don't feel that way about the organization, don't say it. But if you do, it is absurdity not to say so.

Can you pitch company after company and still be sincere about it? Sure. If I were looking for a job in automotive engineering design, I would be delighted to work for any of the four leading automakers.

And I would go to American Motors and say, "You people have been fighting it from the bottom for years — and doing a good job of it. You've come up with a lot of good ideas — like the Pacer — and you're an aggressive company. I want to work for an innovative fighter."

Then I would go to General Motors and say, "You guys have been the leaders as long as anyone can remember, and I want to work for the top cat."

Then I would tell Chrysler, "You people are famous for automotive firsts, engineering breakthroughs like torsion bar suspension and power steering. I want to be in the kind of environment that encourages radical design concepts."

To Ford I would say, "You people have been the leaders in cost-reduction manufacturing techniques, and your marketing has always been imaginative. You have the kind of outfit I'd really like to go to work for."

What I have said in each case is true. I really would like to work for any one of them and for the reasons I gave. I haven't misrepresented myself in any of those instances.

Begging

Some people feel that telling an employer that they really want to work for his organization is begging. It's not. To say "I really want to go to work for you" is a sincere expression of interest. To say "Please give me a job" is begging.

Many job candidates do make the mistake of begging. Students often say something like, "Mr. Recruiter, I'm getting toward the end of the semester. I've had several other interviews, and they don't seem to be panning out very well. It's going to be very important to me to have a job at the end of the semester, and I hope you look on me favorably." The recruiter will most assuredly not look favorably on that candidate. A student recently told a recruiter in my placement center that it was his ninth interview and he hadn't had any bites yet. The recruiter later told me that the student obviously was starting to panic and that it showed in his interview. "He's coming off a loser," the recruiter said.

That recruiter's job is to hire winners, not losers. Examples of losers abound.

On one occasion, when I was a recruiter, I was interviewing a woman for a secretarial job and was quite impressed with her. She was likable and intelligent, and the interview was going well. I was about 10 seconds away from telling her, "You're hired," when she suddenly began to cry. She said, "Mr. Stanat (sob), I've been to (sob) so many (sob) places in the (sob, sob) last two weeks, and I (sob) just can't find a job...." She didn't get that one either. All she had to do was keep that smile on her face and that stiff upper lip for another 10 seconds and she would have had the job. But she crumbled, and she came across as a loser.

I know a man who lost his specialized public contact job when his employer sold the business. The man went broke, declared bankruptcy, and took a part-time sales job that didn't pay much money. Meanwhile he tried to find another job in his field. He had a terrible time because he was down. He sounded down. He looked down. He seemed to sag, and he had a hang-dog expression.

In job interviews, he started begging. He said things like, "Boy, do I ever need this job." Employers are not going to hire someone who says he *needs* a job. They'll hire someone who *wants* a job.

He would say, "I can't make it on my part-time job. I'm not making enough money. I might as well go on relief." Many employers would think, "Go apply for relief. We're not in the social welfare business. The county is."

After a long and frustrating search, he found a job in his field. But it was not a good job.

Don't beg.

TIP: While you should appear eager to get the job you are applying for, you should not appear *over*eager or *over*anxious. That is a tough balance to strike, but you should examine your own personality and figure out at what point your style shifts from eager to *over*eager. When you appear *over*eager, you relinquish your power. Instead of coming off as someone the recruiter might need, you come off as someone who needs the recruiter.

Selling Yourself

Perhaps the most ticklish problem you have in a job interview is getting across to the recruiter the idea that you are good without coming off as an egomaniac. However you **must** get that idea across. It requires tact, poise, sophistication, and persuasive ability. There are people who say, "I'm the greatest," and sometimes they are. Muhammad Ali has said it for years, and he has proved it.

In 1920, H.L. Mencken and George Jean Nathan were co-editors of *The Smart Set,* a magazine that published a lot of important literary criticism. Mencken was the most influential literary critic in the country. One night Mencken and Nathan went to a party at a friend's apartment in New York. They walked in and were accosted by a tall, redheaded drunk. The stranger put one of his arms around

Mencken's neck and the other around Nathan's neck and roared, "So you guys are critics, are you? Well, let me tell you something. I'm the best goddam writer in this here goddam country, and if you, Georgie, and you, Hank, don't know it, you'll know it goddam soon." He pressed them to praise him in *The Smart Set*.

Mencken and Nathan cleared out of the party after only a half hour, mostly to get away from the bellowing redhead.

The next day the manuscript of a novel the redhead had written arrived at Mencken's office. Mencken almost pitched it in the wastebasket, but he remembered that he had nothing to read on a train ride to Baltimore. Mencken read the manuscript and was thunderstruck. He wrote to Nathan: "Grab hold of your barrail, steady yourself, and prepare for a terrible shock! I've just read the advance sheets of the book that lump we met at Schmidt's wrote, and, by God, he has done the job! It's a genuinely excellent piece of work."

The redhead's name was Sinclair Lewis. The novel was *Main Street*.

Ali and Lewis got a chance to back up their boasts. And you can, too. But don't blow your chance by unloading to the recruiter about what a hotshot you are the moment you sit down. You'll get your chance. Give the recruiter time to warm up to you before you tout your talent.

When it comes to selling yourself, you have two ways to go:

• You can, at some point in the interview, flatly tell the recruiter you are good. Some people are comfortable doing that; others are not. I would have no trouble telling a recruiter, "I'm a good history teacher. I prepare my lessons, and I make my classes stimulating. I put out solid material and I work in the colorful information that makes history interesting to kids, and not just a meaningless list of names, dates, and movements. I read every good book on history I can find."

• If you are uncomfortable with the idea of stating flatly that you're good, or if you don't have a track record in the area you're applying for, you can follow up one of the recruiter's questions.

If you are applying for an entry level sales job, for example, the recruiter might ask you, "What makes you think you would be good at sales?" Then you can jump in with both feet and say, "Because I enjoy dealing with different personalities on a continuing basis. Also, there have been some things in my background that indicate that I can be persuasive. For example, I was president of my sorority, and I found that I didn't have to beat people over the head to get things done; I found that people would respond to thoughtful persuasion. Furthermore, I have a lot of self-discipline. I'll get out of bed at seven to make calls on a cold, rainy Wednesday morning without anybody prodding me."

When you've been in a field for a while and are changing jobs, you can point to your victories. When I was a recruiter, my standard questions to salesmen included, "What new accounts have you cracked recently?"

That question gave candidates a magnificent opportunity to tell me how good and how imaginative they were.

Your Defeats

"What were some of your defeats?" is a standard question recruiters ask of experienced people. You should answer the question and, if you can, come up with a positive defense for your defeats.

For example, if you manage a medium-sized hotel and are interviewing for a job as manager of a big hotel, tell about how your efforts increased the occupancy rate 27 percent. Or, if business fell off, explain why: "The owners decided that they were going to milk the operation for maximum profit, and I wasn't left with enough money for proper maintenance. Eventually we became dog-eared and lost some business."

> **TIP:** An obvious point: if the recruiter doesn't ask you about your defeats, don't advertise them.

The wise candidate applying for a job for which he or she has no experience will do a lot of investigation to find out what general qualities and particular skills are needed for the job. That information can be incorporated in a sales pitch. The candidate applying for a job in hospital administration can say:

> I feel comfortable dealing with highly skilled people such as doctors and nurses. I relate well to people who have had a lot of education. I know there has to be a lot of diplomacy in this job, and I am comfortable dealing with people with diverse skills. I know how to deal with the press, and I understand the legislative process. When relevant issues come before the state legislature, I know how to work the machinery to get the hospital's point of view across.

Or for a drafting job, you can say:

> Maybe a lot of people think that sitting at a drafting board all day is constraining. I don't. I get a great kick out of seeing something clean and neat evolve on this piece of paper, particularly when I know it's going to be made into hardware. You're going to find that I'm the one who stays at the board rather than the one who strolls around the plant or gazes out the window.

If it's getting late in the interview and the recruiter hasn't given you an entree into your sales pitch, then you should take the initiative. You can open by saying something such as, "Mr. Recruiter, we've talked quite a bit about this job, and on the basis of what I know about the work and your company, I am more than confident that I can give you what you're looking for and maybe a lot more. There are a lot of jobs I wouldn't say that about, but this job is just right for me." Then elaborate on why you want to work for the organization and why you're good.

A Tough Question

Don't be surprised if a recruiter asks you what your biggest fault is. There are several reasons why he might ask that question:

• To see how candid you will be.

• To see how skillful you are at answering a tough question.

• To get information that will help him disqualify you. Remember, the recruiter has to protect himself. If you have a grievous fault, he wants to know what it is.

• To give himself another weapon to defend you when he describes you to the department manager.

You should be ready for that question. You should not lie, but your answer should present your flaw in the most positive light possible.

No Market for Messiahs

In *What Color Is Your Parachute?* Richard Bolles suggests this approach: spend some time visiting the company as a researcher or observer, find out what the corporate problems are, and then — when you get around to asking for a job — tell the hiring agent how you can solve some of those problems.

That approach might work — but be careful. In general, organizations are not looking for messiahs. Usually what they want is somebody who can do a good job in a clearly defined position. That doesn't mean that organizations aren't receptive to proposals for change, but many executives are wary of self-proclaimed saviors.

A few years ago, a newspaperman with a year and one-half experience at one of the top ten newspapers in the country quit his job and went to graduate school. While he was there, he read the local medium-sized daily newspaper every day. At that time the paper was a journalistic atrocity (it has improved since). The writing was outrageous, and the headlines were illiterate and often inaccurate. The paper's coverage of just about everything — features, government, the university — was inadequate.

The young newsman assembled a thorough and thoughtful booklet, detailing the more grievous offenses that the paper had committed in a week. He gave examples of terrible headlines and showed how better headlines could be written for the stories. One story, for example, was about a debate in medical circles over whether doctors should tell terminal hospital patients that they were going to die. Doctors in England, the story said, felt that the patients should not be told. The paper's headline on the story was "Patient Anxiety Feeds on Hospital, Medic Secrecy." In his booklet, the young man suggested, "Tell Patient He Will Die? British Doctors Say No," a headline that gives a better idea of what the story is about.

Then the young man made an appointment with the publisher of the paper, a man of about 70, to discuss the paper, show him the booklet, and ask for a high-level job, such as assistant managing editor.

The old man talked to him for about five minutes, refused to look at the booklet, and curtly showed him to the door. Maybe he didn't know the paper was bad, and maybe he didn't care. The paper was making money. And he didn't want any 25-year-old saviors. Maybe the young man could have gotten some sort of editorship at the paper. He certainly had the talent for the job. But he alienated the publisher with a stiff attack on the publisher's product.

You can knock yourself out of a job by jumping all over somebody's creation. I did once. Several years ago, I applied to be director of personnel for a national corporation. I went through several interviews and was doing very well. The last interview was with the corporation president.

We had a good conversation. Before I left, he handed me a stack of papers and said, "We're thinking about installing this retirement program for key individuals. You say you have had experience with retirement programs. Look that over and give me your response."

I knew that my comments on the program were the key to getting or losing the job. I took the plan home, looked it over, and typed up a three-page report. I went back to the president and said, "This retirement plan is terrible. Parts of it are illegal and the funding in parts of it is badly defined." I went through it step by step and tore it apart.

I did not get the job. The president had written the plan himself.

If I had asked him who had written it before I took it home, I would have realized that I would have to be diplomatic about any criticism of the program. If I had said, "This plan is super. I suppose that if you run it through some legal people, there might be some minor changes they'd want to make here and there. But this concept here is terrific, and that concept is forward looking," I probably would have gotten the job.

I would not have gone so far as to tell him that the plan was "super" because I thought it was a bad plan, but I would have told him that more delicately. People are most sensitive about two things: their kids and their own creations.

Item H

Heads Up

Keep your wits about you. Careless errors can knock you out of consideration for any job, particularly when you have competition.

A few years ago a student raised hell with me and my staff at the university placement center because we couldn't find his folder. He insisted that he had registered with us, so we spent several hours combing our files.

Eventually we found his folder and discovered what had happened. When the young man filled out his registration form, he failed to read the instruction that said "last name first." So where he was supposed to write his last name, he wrote his first name, "Peter." Then he apparently started to read the form because where it said "first name," he complied and wrote in "Peter." We filed him as Peter Peter.

When you fill out application forms, people aren't going to ask you to verify such things as your name. Employers expect you to be capable of telling them who you are, so get your personal data correct on applications and resumes.

The number of job seekers who make mistakes writing down their phone number is astonishing. Recruiters won't chase you very far. If you make a mistake in listing your phone number on an application, you will have destroyed the confidence the recruiter might have had in you. Many recruiters wouldn't even pick up the phone book to learn your correct number. One recruiter said recently that one-third of the applicants at his company are untraceable.

For several years, I was the chief recruiter for the Louis Allis Company, a manufacturer of motors, located in Milwaukee. On the other side of town was the Allis-Chalmers Corporation, referred to in newspaper headlines as A-C. Down the road from the Louis Allis plant was the AC Spark Plug Division of General Motors.

This was just too much of a muddle for quite a few candidates. People who were supposed to be interviewing with me at Louis Allis occasionally showed up at Allis-Chalmers. AC Spark Plug drew stray Allis-Chalmers candidates, and Allis-Chalmers drew sleepy candidates for jobs at both other companies.

A mistake like that can knock a recruiter's day haywire. Recruiters sometimes work on a tight schedule. If I had a 9:00 A.M. appointment with a candidate in my office, I would expect him to be there at 9:00. When it got to be 9:10 and he wasn't there, my opinion of him hit the bottom. And if I got a call at 9:15 from the recruiter at Allis-Chalmers saying, "Hey, Kirby, I've got one of yours," I'd know that the rest of my morning would be screwed up because by the time the guy drove or took a cab across town it would be close to 10:00 before the interview got underway. No matter how good the candidate was, an interview like that was always off to a stumbling start. It's difficult for a candidate to recover from that kind of blunder.

Even candidates who were in the right place would get their wires crossed. I had more than one Louis Allis candidate tell me, "I've always wanted to work here because my grandfather had one of your tractors." Louis Allis makes motors. Allis-Chalmers makes tractors.

Students often operate in incredible information voids. Recently a worried student came into my office. A recruiter for a paper company had promised to call him within a week. Two weeks had gone by, and the recruiter hadn't called. The kid wanted to call the recruiter, *but he didn't know his name*; he only knew the name of the company. Fortunately, I knew who the recruiter was.

Students are constantly coming into the placement office and saying to a secretary, "I have an interview today. I made a note of it here on my calendar. But I can't remember who it's with."

You should make sure you have complete information at every step. Take notes. Ask questions. If the recruiter introduces himself to you as John Mumblemumble, with the last name coming at you as a mish-mash of consonants, ask him during the interview to pronounce his name again. And he'll tell you, "John Schleuterman." Ask him to spell it. Write it down. Then, later in the interview, don't call him Mr. Schlichterberg."

Stay awake. Don't make stupid mistakes.

12

SECOND INTERVIEWS

Maintain your head of steam

When you graduate to a second interview, you're hot. You should get the job. The statistics prove it. Ninety percent of the college seniors who take second interviews with IBM get a job offer. At the Shell Oil Company in Houston, 80 percent of the nonprofessionals who get second interviews get job offers. A recruiter at Shell explained, "We like to think we know our business and that we can screen people. Most of the people we send to the department heads get hired."

In the second interview you have several things going for you that you didn't have in the first interview.

• In most cases, you have less competition, maybe none at all.

• You have the assurance that the employer is interested in you, so you are on much firmer ground than in the first interview.

• Most important, you have the benediction of the recruiter. You have an ally who has a stake in your getting hired. When I was a recruiter, if I invited a candidate to meet a department manager, I fully expected that individual to get a job offer. The only time I would ever take a candidate without my full support to a manager was when that manager had been on my back saying, "Show me somebody, show me somebody, show me somebody," and I didn't have anybody good enough to show him. In that situation, I would present the best of the poor candidates. That candidate was on solid ground, too, because while the manager knew that I wasn't enthusiastic about the candidate, he also knew that the candidate was the best of the lot.

Whenever the recruiter recommends you to a manager, the recruiter is saying to the manager, in effect, "You ought to hire this person. I'm willing to stand beside you and take the blame if he doesn't work out." If that understanding between the recruiter and the manager did not exist, the recruiter would, in effect, be saying to the manager, "I have a candidate for the job in your department, but I can't recommend that you hire him. If you do, it's going to be your own hook. If he doesn't work out, you're going to stand alone." That's similar to my presenting the best of the poor candidates to pacify an eager manager. If situations like that were the rule and not the exception, there would be very little need for recruiters.

When managers reject recruiters' candidates, the recruiters tend to blame the managers. Whenever that happened to me, I felt the manager was narrow-minded, ignorant, or guilty of giving me the wrong specifications. That's how recruiters think.

The relationship between recruiters and managers in big organizations frequently is such that the first interview is "hard screen" and the second interview is merely a verification. It is a verification by the manager that the recruiter is accurate in concluding that the candidate is good. It amounts to the recruiter saying to the manager, "Charlie, if you think she's as good an accountant as I do, she's all yours." And the manager says, "Okay."

Knowing that, you can go into the second interview confident that you are strong.

Second Interviews Vary

You can never be sure what kind of second interview you are going to have:

• It can be with one manager, the head of the department you would be working in. That manager, either on his own or after consultation with the recruiter, will decide whether to hire you or not.

• It can be with the manager and the recruiter.

• It can be with the same person you had your first interview with. (Maybe your first interview was with a manager instead of a personnel specialist, and he wants to take another look.)

• It can be with several managers, either one at a time or in a group. You might talk to the head of the department and with lower level supervisors.

• Your second interview might be with a supervisor, the person who heads the section of the department you would be working in. The supervisor might take you into the department head's office for another inspection. The department head probably won't have much to do with deciding whether or not you get the job. His attitude will probably be, "If you (the supervisor) like him, he's okay with me." You should be aware, though, that while the boss probably won't be heavily involved in the hiring decision, he does have kill power. So don't spit on his carpet or comment on the fact that he's going bald.

• It can be with a special committee.

• The second interview can be a series of interviews with the same manager or managers. That usually means you're in a close race with other candidates or that the employer is being supercautious and wants to be extra sure about you.

Several days or weeks might pass before you are called in for a second interview. (At the end of your first interview, you should have asked the recruiter when you will hear from him. If he said it would be within two weeks, wait two weeks and a day and then call him.) When you interview with a recruiter at a college placement center, there generally will be a wait of at least several days and sometimes weeks before you get called to the company's office for a second interview. The recruiter usually wants to look over the field before he chooses his candidates. If during an interview at the placement center you get invited in for a second interview, you are a strong candidate.

When you do missionary work, answer a newspaper ad, or use an employment agency, you might talk to the recruiter for 10 or 15 minutes and then be catapulted right into the second interview. The recruiter might say, "I'd like to take you down the hall to meet Dan Clark, who is in charge of Accounts Receivable." Wham! You're into it. The recruiter may leave you in his own office for a few minutes while he goes down the hall to pitch you to Clark. And he may not. He may just call Clark to see if Clark can spare a few minutes. In either case, you have the recruiter's blessing. The mere fact that the recruiter is taking you to Clark almost always means that you have his support. You have struck your allegiance.

Competition

Sometimes you will be the only candidate sent to the manager for the second interview. You can't beat those odds.

Sometimes two or three other candidates will be sent to the manager. The decision on which one of you is to be hired will not be made on the basis of qualifications. All of you are qualified for the job. If you are applying for an engineering job, and three other candidates are going in for second interviews, all four of you are engineers. The manager might do some scratching to try to figure out which of you is best, but he probably won't be able to get a firm handle on that. The most important factor will be body chemistry.

One college recruiter for a manufacturing company used to use psychology on managers when his company planned to hire 8 or 10 people at a time. He knew that even if he brought in 10 Nobel Prize winners, there was no chance that all 10 would be hired. The managers didn't want to look too indiscriminate. Besides, if they hired 10 out of 10, they knew the recruiter would get a big head. So the recruiter would feed them some people to turn down. He'd bring in 10 outstanding candidates he had interviewed on the college circuit and 2 obvious losers. (The losers were always local. The recruiter didn't want to pay travel expenses for people who couldn't even add.) The managers would be impressed by the crop. They'd hire the 10 strong candidates and turn down the losers. Every once in a while, though, somebody would make an offer to one of the losers. That always left the recruiter thinking, "How the hell did that happen?"

The Dynamics of the Second Interview

In the second interview, all of the body chemistry that operated in the first interview is still the prime factor. The manager has to like you. And you owe the second interviewer the same four things you owed the recruiter: a professional attitude and appearance, a knowledge of the company, a clear idea of what you want to do, and a pitch.

A poor manager will make little or no attempt to find out how good you are. A good manager will try his absolute best to find out. But any good manager knows that *he'll never know for sure until you go to work in his department*. There is no foolproof way to find out ahead of time.

What does he have to go on?

• Your experience? The best companies in the world have incompetents on the payroll. The fact that a candidate is working at Xerox is no guarantee that he's a star.

• References and recommendations? They can be helpful to the manager, but they are hearsay. And managers know that candidates don't list hostile references.

• Samples of your work? In some fields, such as architecture and illustrating, samples can be helpful to the manager. But making a hiring decision on the basis of samples has drawbacks. The first-rate sketch that an illustrator shows might have taken him three days, instead of the three hours it should have taken. That architect's plans might be the result of a committee effort or might have gone through 10 costly revisions. Newspaper editors want to see samples of stories written by candidates for reporting jobs. But editors know that a reporter can write gibberish and a skillful copy editor can turn it into a good story. They know that what came out in print might not have been what came out of the reporter's typewriter.

• The candidate's ability to express himself about the work? That can be a major factor in the manager's decision. A good manager might tear you apart to find out how much you know about the field and how you feel about various aspects of the work. But he knows that good talkers are often lousy doers.

You should be prepared to satisfy a manager in all of these areas: be ready to present your work in as positive a way as you can, carry strong references, be armed with good samples of your work (if it's the kind of job that would involve showing samples), and spend some time before the interview reviewing your general thoughts on the field and on some particular aspects of the job.

The manager will probably consider all of these factors. But he knows that none of them is scientific proof of ability. All of these factors will contribute to his total *impression* of you. It is that *total impression* that will determine whether you get hired or not. And impressions are based mostly on body chemistry.

The Offer

There are only three likely ways for the second interview to end:

• You are told that they will get in touch with you.

• You are asked to return for a third interview (which is really an extension of the second interview.)

• You get an offer.

It is rare for candidates who make it to the second interview to be rejected on the spot. It is far less embarrassing for everyone when the employer does it by mail.

If the manager tells you that either he or the recruiter will let you know whether you got the job, ask when you should expect to get the word. If it is more than a day, you should go home and immediately write a brief letter to the manager. Send a copy of the letter to the recruiter. Your letter should talk about how much you enjoyed the interview and should reaffirm your interest in the organization and in the job. If the manager is having a tough time deciding between you and two other candidates, your letter might tip the decision in your favor. (Remember, you always have to maximize your chances.) Consider what might happen if you don't send a letter: the other two candidates might write letters, which would make you odd-person-out. Don't mail your letter at the corner mailbox. Take it to your local post office and mail it there so that it gets there fast. But don't send it special delivery — that will make you seem overeager.

As with the first interview, wait the amount of time the employer told you it would take for him to get back to you plus one working day. If you don't get the word, get on the phone.

If you get an offer during the second interview (or, for that matter, during the first interview), you can either reject it on the spot, accept it and get out of this mess called job hunting, or ask for some time to think it over.

Don't ask for time unless you really need it. If the offer is what you want, take it. But if you have to talk it over with your family, or compute such things as how the salary you were offered will work with your budget, you are certainly within your rights to ask for some time. If you do, you should specify how much time you want: "I'll let you know this afternoon," or, "I'll get back to you by Friday." You should also take care to assure the employer that you really are serious about the job.

Sometimes an employer will insist on an answer on the spot. If you don't want to give your answer immediately and the employer refuses to budge, you're in a power poker game. You then have to make your decision based on the particulars of your own situation. If you want the job, take it. If it is *absolutely impossible* for you to make a decision on the spot, you have no choice but to reject the offer. In many cases, if you reject the offer, the employer will back down and give you some time to consider. Employers don't want to be turned down any more than you do. It's a defeat, and sometimes it means they have to start the costly process all over again.

Item I

Testing

After you have hand-delivered your resume to the recruiter, after the recruiter has picked your brains in an exhaustive interview, and after you've survived a confrontation with the department head and have been cleared in a reference check, your ordeal may not be over. You may be put through psychological tests, which could take several hours or several days. (You may take tests at any point in the hiring process, as standard operating procedures vary from company to company and from job to job.)

The likelihood that you will be tested is less than it used to be. Title VII of the Civil Rights Act states that in most cases employers cannot use tests that routinely eliminate minority group candidates. Tests must be validated by research to show that they honestly relate to work performance and do not discriminate against minorities. Preparation and validation of these tests is time consuming and can cost from $25,000 to $250,000.

Rather than go through the hassle, some employers are cutting back on their testing programs. They still give shorthand and typing tests to secretaries, but they hesitate to give general intelligence tests. Several Supreme Court decisions, including *Griggs* v. *Duke Power Company* (1971), in which the power company required a high school education or a certain score on an intelligence test, have contributed to this reticence. Duke Power Company lost its case. The test or diploma requirement was determined to be a nonrelevant criterion for job performance.

When testing is used, it can take many forms. You could (despite the Duke case) face tests that measure your IQ; tests that measure specific ability, such as mechanical skill; tests that show your range of interests; or personality tests such as the Rorschach inkblot tests which explore your psychological makeup.

Which specific test are you likely to face? It's hard to say, since there are over 2,500 tests that can be used to screen job candidates.

Testing is done in different ways. You may be sent to a consulting industrial psychologist for an evaluation. You may first be tested on a group of traits the employer wants all employees to have. Then you may be tested for the group of traits the employer thinks are necessary for the job you are applying for. Kelly Conrad, psychologist with Humber, Mundie & McClary, listed some of the traits his group commonly measures:

• Impact — the ability to create a good impression, to command attention

• Energy — Will the candidate attack a problem or snooze over it?

• Oral Communication Skills — including gestures and nonverbal communication

• Written Communication Skills

• Creativity — Does the candidate have imagination?

• Range of Interests

• Stress Tolerance — Will the candidate turn to marmalade under pressure?

• Motivation — Does the candidate take satisfaction in work?

• Work Standards — Will the candidate do a good job for its own sake?

• Career Ambition — Does the candidate have a self-development program?

• Leadership Ability

• Sensitivity — Does the candidate respond to the feelings of other people?

Some traits that are measured in potential managers are the ability to plan and organize; management controls; the use of delegation; problem analysis; judgment; and, decisiveness.

Some companies don't farm their candidates out to consulting psychologists; they have the psychologist design testing programs that are administered in-house. You might find yourself in company headquarters going through a three-day session with other candidates. Perhaps you will come up against a simulation test, such as "in-basket," which is a technique used by some employers to simulate on-the-job performance. Here is how "in-basket" might be explained to you:

> A department manager has been called away
> unexpectedly. You have been asked to fill in for

the manager. But you have some problems. You only have three hours to do the work, and you can't consult with anybody else because it's Saturday and everybody else in the company is on the golf course. See the in-basket? There is a pile of memos that list problems you must solve, and you must write your solutions down. You have three hours. Good luck.

Or you might find yourself sitting around a table with five other candidates for the job. You will be told that you have a million dollars in company funds to allocate and that you will be given a general description of where the company is. You and your fellow candidates will sit and haggle over possible solutions, while three department managers are lounging in the background with their arms crossed, observing your performance.

All of this makes some people very nervous. There are candidates who go through an afternoon of testing having to go to the bathroom but not having the nerve to ask. Some applicants sit sweating in their jackets but are afraid to take them off.

Candidates who get shook up don't perform well. If you have some problem that may affect your performance — such as cracking up the car on the way to the testing — you should tell whoever is in charge.

Conrad says that there are ways for you to increase your performance in testing. He suggests:

• Your testing skills may be rusty, but you can sharpen them by doing practice tests, such as those in the College Entrance Examination test books.

• If you are weak in communication skills, you should launch a reading program. Read business magazines, such as *Fortune*, and look up the words you don't know. Lack of communication skills, by the way, is the most common reason why candidates do poorly on tests. One candidate, a manager, was questioned why his test performance was so poor when he seemed to be communicating well on the job. "I give all of my written work to my secretary to do," he explained.

• Think about your job history before you go into the tests. You most certainly will be asked what was satisfying and dissatisfying about your past jobs or your present job.

• Think about what your plans and goals are. Ask yourself why you are applying for the job and where you want to be in five years.

• Try not to get too uptight about the testing. Be willing to present yourself as fairly and as openly as possible.

• Get a good rest before you take the tests.

If you have reached the middle management level and feel that you are going to have to undergo tests when you apply for a job, you can prepare yourself by having an industrial psychologist administer a typical set of tests to you. You can learn where your weaknesses and strengths are and work on them. Of course, having a psychologist test you is going to cost some money.

After you go through testing ordered by a potential employer, you may or may not get the results. Some companies and psychologists have an open information policy, and some do not. If you are rejected on the basis of your test performance, you would be wise to ask the company how you failed. If you do well on the tests and get the job, you don't have to ask for test results. You can just gloat.

13

QUALIFICATIONS

Make the most of what counts

Hiring decisions are not based on qualifications. They never have been, and they probably never will be. The purpose of this chapter is to offer further evidence that the major factor in hiring is body chemistry — the image the candidate projects, the vibrations the candidate emits — charisma, not qualifications.

In my job as campus placement director, I occasionally visit companies to keep abreast of trends in entry level hiring. In the placement center, I talk mostly with recruiters, but on my visits to company offices, I meet managers. I recently visited the headquarters of an insurance company.

The first person I talked to was the head of the systems group, which handles system analysis, programming, and all the other functions of the company's massive computer operation. I asked the manager what sort of entry level people he was looking for.

"The people we seek," he said, "could be in computer science, math, applied math, and physics." But, he said, he was interested in talking with *all majors*, and he added that, more than anything, he was interested in "candidates who are alert, know what they want, and sell themselves." He said he is not too concerned about a candidate's grade point. He felt that he could decide for himself, on the basis on an interview, whether or not the candidate is sharp.

178

The manager said he had recently promoted his best systems analyst, a woman he had hired right off the campus. She was an *art* major with no computer experience. I asked him why he hired an art major. Because, he said, he could tell from the way she handled herself in the interview that she was intelligent. He said she impressed him as somebody who "wanted a future" and as somebody who wouldn't need a lot of supervision. He said he pegged her as hard working and organized in her approach to a task.

Does that manager really want a science major or a math major? Yes, he does. But he'll talk to anyone, and he'll hire someone who impresses him.

I went from the computer area to the Claims Department. Those are the people you deal with when you smash up your car or when your house burns down.

The manager said they hire entry level people with any major. He did not mention grade point. He indicated that he was interested in people who are sales types— outgoing and able to deal with other people.

I asked him, "Would this be the kind of person you'd like to go fishing with?"

He looked at me and said, "Yes. That's who I want."

Then I went to the Employee Benefit Department. These are the people who work with major corporations that have health and accident plans for their employees. They, too, talk to all majors. They would prefer a business major or someone who has taken some business courses, but that's not critical. They said they prefer people who have taken math courses, but when I started to probe into that, it became clear that they meant simple arithmetic — adding, subtracting, multiplying and dividing — not calculus. They want an extrovert, with a sales personality, someone who is attracted to people and vice-versa. "Somebody you would like to go fishing with?" I asked the manager. "Yes," he said, "I guess that's the one I'm after."

The next stop was the Property Underwriting Department. People in that department handle such things as assessing the value of a building and its contents, setting a rate on insuring the building, and writing a policy.

The Underwriting manager said he doesn't care what entry level candidates major in. Average grades are acceptable. He wants to talk to candidates who are geographically flexible, who are impressive, and who like to get out and hustle new business. Somebody he'd like to go fishing with? Sure.

The last manager I met was the head of the Casualty Underwriting Department. He stressed compatibility. He said he looks for people who can blend with his unit. He also said he wants people who are highly motivated, who are able to communicate, who have good potential, and who are alert and inquisitive. He wants people who are interested in business, but he doesn't demand that they be business majors. He, too, agreed that he was interested in people he would like to go fishing with.

That company is a highly successful one, with a low employee turnover rate. (And it's not because they do a lot of fishing or engage in a lot of other social niceties.)

I spent a full working day talking to the managers. Not one mentioned the word *qualifications*. They said, essentially, "Send me bright, aggressive, compatible people, and we will train them."

One manager told me that "at the end of five minutes I'd just as soon cut the (job) interview off. After that, I'm not going to learn anything more that's really meaningful to me. After five minutes, I know whether I'm going to go with this individual or not."

Body chemistry is paramount at all levels. It is operating when an automobile manufacturing company's directors decide which vice-president will be promoted to president, when a university conducts a nationwide search for a new president, and when voters decide who will be president.

Grades

Except for the degree graduating seniors are going to receive and their major field of study, their grade point average is just about the only credential they have. Some recruiters have no interest whatsoever in a candidate's grades. Others consider grades important. But a candidate can almost always overcome low grades by having good body chemistry.

Consider two candidates, male or female. Candidate A has a pleasing personality; a warm smile; an assured manner; the ability to answer questions thoughtfully; a brisk walk; neat, well-fitting clothes; a squeaky-clean look; and a 2.2 average (A=4.0).

Candidate B is dull and unfriendly; seems ill at ease; mumbles vague answers; slouches; is dressed in dowdy clothes; looks a little grubby; and has a 3.8. I'll bet on Candidate A every time.

Good grades are important. They definitely can help you get a job. But I have yet to meet the recruiter who said that just because a student has a 3.7, he or she automatically has the job.

A straight A average would seem to be a ticket to a job with almost any employer. But a straight A bothers many recruiters. Students with a 4 point sometimes are asked unusual questions, such as, "What have you done with your spare time?" or "When was the last time you had a date?" or "What are your plans for marriage?" or "Do you play cards?" or "What kind of dancing do you like?" Some recruiters assume that an A average is the result of four years in a garret, with no social contact.

For the 1976 *Endicott Report* recruiters were surveyed on what criteria they used when considering entry level applicants. The report on that study is in Table 13–1.

Body chemistry comes out on top. Grades are second.

TABLE 13-1

IMPORTANT FACTORS IN THE SELECTION OF COLLEGE GRADUATES FOR EMPLOYMENT

Of special interest to college students, parents, faculty members, and counselors is the relative importance of various factors employers consider in selecting college graduates for employment. In other words, how do recruiters determine which applicants are best qualified?

Respondents to this year's inquiry were asked to rank, in order of importance, six factors commonly considered by employers in the selection of college graduates. Responding employers ranked the six factors from 1 to 6, with 1 representing greatest importance.

It was noted in tabulating the responses that some employers ranked certain factors high and others ranked them lower. The average rankings in the following table are, therefore, only general indications of relative importance.

FACTORS CONSIDERED IN THE EMPLOYMENT OF COLLEGE AND UNIVERSITY GRADUATES	FIELDS OF STUDY IN COLLEGE							
	ENGINEERING AND OTHER TECHNICAL		ACCOUNTING AND BUS. ADMIN.		LIBERAL ARTS AND OTHER NON TECH.		ALL FIELDS OF STUDY	
	Order	Average Rank	Order	Average Rank	Order	Average Rank	Order	Average Rank
Personal qualifications, including maturity, initiative, enthusiasm, poise, appearance, and the ability to work with people.	(1)	1.97	(1)	1.73	(1)	1.52	(1)	1.75
Scholastic qualifications as shown by grades in all subjects or in a major field.	(2)	2.37	(2)	2.43	(2)	2.64	(2)	2.47
Specialized courses relating to particular field of work.	(3)	2.72	(3)	3.07	(5)	3.99	(3)	3.22
Kind and amount of part-time or summer employment while in college.	(4)	3.72	(4)	3.89	(4)	3.85	(4)	3.82
Experience in campus activities, especially leadership and participation in extracurricular life.	(5)	4.31	(5)	3.94	(3)	3.60	(5)	3.96
General or liberal arts courses designed to provide a broad cultural background.	(6)	5.54	(6)	5.41	(6)	5.05	(6)	5.35
Number of companies responding		166		190		146		215

Some Recruiter Reactions

For years I have been calling recruiters in at the end of their day of interviewing candidates at my campus placement center. I ask them which students fell down and how. For several weeks last year I made notes on recruiters' comments. Here are my notes (the types of firms the recruiters represented are in parentheses, and the recruiters' comments follow):

- A male student (recruiter from a manufacturing company)—The recruiter's comment: No coat.
- A male (an accounting firm)—Has no idea where he is going. Doesn't know what he wants to do. Eight-ball.
- A male (a retail firm)—Appearance bad. Hair was too long and unwashed. Poor communication.
- A male (a bank)—Hair too long.
- A female (an insurance company)—No diction.
- A male (an accounting firm)—Really disappointed in him. Was like he was dead when he was in there. Unpleasant.
- A male (a manufacturing company)—Needs a haircut.
- A male (a manufacturing company)— Clammed up. Couldn't get anything out of him.
- A male (a manufacturing company)—Tough to open him up. Should be more aggressive.
- A male (a retail firm)—Hair too long.
- A male (an accounting firm)—Grooming. Shirttail out.
- A male (a manufacturing company)—Said absolutely nothing. Doesn't sell himself. No questions.
- A female (manufacturing company)— Initially overwhelmed me with documentation.

- A female (an accounting firm)—More enthusiasm.
- A female (an accounting firm)—Tense. Didn't relax until the end.
- A male (an accounting firm)—Poor eye contact.
- A male (an accounting firm)—Needs to talk more. Difficult to get a good discussion.
- A female (an accounting firm)—"Stiff as a board." Didn't have anything to say about herself. Didn't express herself too well.
- A female (an insurance company)—Sharp but no direction. Wants career counseling.
- A male (an accounting firm)—Poorly dressed, not prepared, hadn't read literature, no questions.
- A male (an accounting firm)—Doesn't know what he wants. Weak handshake.
- A male (a lending institution)—Hadn't read material. Didn't know what he wanted to do.
- A female (a lending institution)—No interest in company. "If worse comes to worse, I'll listen."
- A female (a lending institution)—Didn't ask any questions.
- A female (a manufacturing company)—Doesn't define what she wants to do.
- A male (a manufacturing company)—Came on a little too strong. "Give me a chance."
- A male (a manufacturing company)—Resume handwritten.
- A male (a manufacturing company)—Doesn't know what he wants to do.
- A male (a manufacturing company)—No coat or tie.
- A male (a manufacturing company)—Doesn't know what he wants to do. Thinks

he wants advertising but doesn't know what that is.

• A male (a manufacturing company)—Talks too much, example: "Why did I say that? I didn't mean that. I was just kidding."

• A male (a manufacturing company)—Can't talk. Needs to open up.

• A female (a manufacturing company)—Too introverted. Poor eye contact.

• A male (a manufacturing company)—Fine person. Very poor communication skills.

• A male (a transportation company)—"A hippie on pot acting like he really wanted to work." Big mop of untidy hair. "Can't get along with present supervisors (plural)."

• A female (an insurance company)—Her idea of management is off. Management requires more than a house mother.

• A male (a retailer)—Tried to be off-hand. Ended up being caustic. Flip. All-around poor candidate.

• A male (a manufacturing company)—Low grade point bothers him too much. Talks too much about it; defends it too much. Be more positive.

• A male (a manufacturing firm)—Interests too narrow. Only thing he wants to do is open up his own cycle shop and work on them.

Nobody mentioned qualifications: only body chemistry.

Evaluation Forms

Recruiters from most big companies fill out an evaluation form after they have interviewed a candidate. Here are copies of five organizations' evaluation forms. The first four are for private companies. The fifth, a two-page form, is for a unit of government. The names have been removed. These forms should provide some insight into what recruiters want in a candidate.

Again, the emphasis is on body chemistry.

INTERVIEWER'S RATING SHEET

Name of Applicant: _____ Date _____

Candidate For: _____ Interviewer: _____

1. APPEARANCE Very untidy; poor taste in dress.	Somewhat careless about personal appearance.	Satisfactory personal appearance.	Good taste in dress, better than average appearance.	Unusually well groomed, very neat, excellent taste in dress.
2. FRIENDLINESS Appears very distant and aloof.	Approachable; fairly friendly.	Warm, friendly, sociable.	Very sociable and outgoing.	Extremely friendly and sociable.
3. POISE-STABILITY Ill at ease; is "jumpy" and appears nervous.	Somewhat tense.	About as poised as the average applicant.	Sure of self.	Extremely well composed.
4. PERSONALITY Unsatisfactory.	Questionable.	Satisfactory.	Very desirable.	Outstanding.
5. CONVERSATIONAL ABILITY Talks very little; expresses himself poorly.	Tries to express himself but does fair job at best.	Average fluency and expression.	Talks well and "to the point."	Excellent expression; extremely fluent; forceful.
6. ALERTNESS Slow to "catch on."	Rather slow; requires more than average explanation.	Grasps ideas with average ability.	Quick to understand; perceives very well.	Exceptionally keen and alert.
7. INFORMATION ABOUT GENERAL WORK FIELD Poor knowledge of field.	Fair knowledge of field.	Is as informed as the average applicant.	Fairly well informed: knows more than average applicant.	Has excellent knowledge of field.
8. EXPERIENCE No relationship between applicant's background and job requirements.	Fair relationship between applicant's background and job requirements.	Average amount of meaningful background and experience.	Background very good; considerable experience.	Excellent background and experience.
9. DRIVE Has poorly defined goals and appears to act without purpose.	Appears to set goals too low and to put forth little effort to achieve these.	Has reached goals that were set at a moderate level.	Has high goals; worked hard to attain them but fell somewhat short.	Has set high goals and reached or even exceeded them.
10. ATTITUDE TOWARD JOB Just another job; might leave without notice.	Indifferent; interested in pay, location, or some small part of the job.	Not excited about job or company, but might develop interest.	Interested in the company and job; probably prefers it to others.	Extremely interested in the company and the job; completely sold on the organization.
11. OVERALL Definitely unsatisfactory.	Substandard.	Average.	Definitely above average.	Outstanding.

Do you recommend hiring for this job

YES ☐   NO ☐   MAYBE ☐   Explain and Comment _____

_____

_____

_____

APPLICANT APPRAISAL FORM - CAMPUS

NAME OF
APPLICANT _____

COLLEGE OR
UNIVERSITY _____

BEST DAY OF WEEK FOR OFFICE VISIT _____ LOCATION PREFERENCE _____

DO NOT FILL OUT IN PRESENCE OF APPLICANT				
PLEASE EXPRESS YOUR OPINION ON EACH ITEM	MEETS REQUIREMENTS			DOES NOT MEET REQUIRE-MENTS
	OUT-STANDING	ABOVE AVERAGE	SATIS-FACTORY	
1. ORAL COMMUNICATION SKILLS				
2. DESIRABLE SELF-CONFIDENCE				
3. ABILITY TO BE CONVINCING AND GAIN RESPECT				
4. MOTIVATION				
5. LEADERSHIP POTENTIAL				
6. PREPARATION FOR THE INTERVIEW				
7. APPEARANCE (DRESS AND GROOMING)				
8. ACADEMIC PREPARATION: ACCOUNTING				
OTHER SUBJECTS				

THE FOLLOWING COMMENTS ARE INCLUDED TO EXPAND ON THE ABOVE AND TO INCREASE THE EFFECTIVENESS OF THIS APPRAISAL:

_____
_____
_____
_____
_____
_____
_____
_____

REASON FOR LOCATION PREFERENCE IF OTHER THAN LOCAL OFFICE:_____

CONCLUSION:
MY APPRAISAL OF HOW THIS PERSON WILL PERFORM AMONG CONTEMPORARIES DURING THE FIRST YEAR ON OUR STAFF IS:

PLACE AN "X" IN THE APPROPRIATE BOX.

DOES NOT MEET REQUIREMENTS | SATISFACTORY | ABOVE AVERAGE | OUT-STANDING

10% 20% 30% 40% 50% 60% 70% 80% 90%

☐ AUDIT
☐ TAX
☐ PTR. ☐ A/S
☐ MGR. ☐ ADMIN.

NAME _____
(PLEASE PRINT)

REVIEWED BY DIRECTOR OF RECRUITING _____
INITIAL   DATE

CAMPUS INTERVIEW FORM

Candidate's Name	School	Interviewer	Date

CHARACTERISTICS	EVALUATION				
	Outstanding	Above Average	Acceptable	Limited Potential	Not Acceptable
A. APPEARANCE					
B. PREPARATION FOR INTERVIEW Knowledge of firm Knowledge of profession Asked good questions					
C. COMMUNICATIVE ABILITY					
D. DIRECTION Confident Realistic and practical					
E. MATURITY					
F. SINCERITY					
G. PERSONALITY Enthusiastic Industrious Likeable					
H. QUALIFICATIONS Academic preparation Apparent intelligence					
I. OVERALL EVALUATION Long - range potential Drive and ambition Ability					

COMMENTS _____

_____

_____

_____

_____

NUMERICAL RATING IN RELATION TO OTHER CANDIDATES

_____ Office invitation
_____ Uncertain
_____ No interest
_____ Refer to _____ Office

By what date should candidate be contacted? _____

188

INTERVIEWER EVALUATION - CAMPUS

BACKGROUND

Name _____ Nickname _____

College _____ Degree _____ Major _____

Interviewed by _____ Position _____ Date _____

Grades · Overall _____ Major _____

Number of credits in accounting_____

Faculty appraisal _____

Outside interests or activities _ Very Active _____ Participates _____ None _____

Location preference(s)_____

Military obligation _____

EVALUATION

	Excellent	Good	Average	Needs Improvement	Unsatisfactory
Appearance					
Poise					
Oral Expression					
Personality					
Confidence					
Alertness					
Ambition					
Enthusiasm					
Potential for Advancement					

COMMENTS

(Any additional remarks concerning the student and other relevant factors discerned from the interview.)

_____

_____

_____

_____

_____

_____

_____

_____

OUTCOME OF INTERVIEW

_____ Confirm invitation to visit the office   _____ Refer to another office
_____ Extend invitation to visit office   _____ (office)
_____ Defer until next campus visit   _____ Turn down

___ INTERVIEW APPRAISAL WORK SHEET

Name of Applicant

Present Address		City and State		Phone

Marital Status	No. of Children		Major	Minor

Age	College		Graduation Date:	B.S./B.A.	M.A.	Ph.D.

Has this person filed a ___ application and sent it to the Bureau of Personnel?　Yes　No

Has this person written the ___ examination?　Yes　No　Grade Point　Point System

1. GENERAL APPEARANCE
General Physical Appearance. Appropriateness of Clothing. Neatness. Grooming. Cleanliness
☐ Exceptional　☐ Above Average　☐ Average　☐ Below Average　☐ Unsatisfactory

2. POISE · MATURITY
Bearing and Posture. Mannerisms. Physical and Social Ease. Emotional Stability and Balance. Flexibility and Confidence.
☐ Exceptional　☐ Above Average　☐ Average　☐ Below Average　☐ Lacking

3. ATTITUDE · ADAPTABILITY
Personal Philosophy and Outlook. Sense of Responsibility. Open-mindedness. Cooperation. Mental and Social Adaptability. Attitude towards Authority.
☐ Exceptional　☐ Above Average　☐ Average　☐ Below Average　☐ Poor

4. LEADERSHIP QUALITIES
Personal Forcefulness. Ability to Inspire Confidence. Participation in Leadership Activities. Organizational Ability.
☐ Exceptional　☐ Above Average　☐ Average　☐ Below Average　☐ Lacking

5. COMMUNICATION SKILL
Ability of Self Expression. Method and Manner of Speech. Voice Quality. Organization of Thoughts.
☐ Exceptional　☐ Above Average　☐ Average　☐ Below Average　☐ Unsatisfactory

6. INITIATIVE · RESOURCEFULNESS
Industrious. Vigor. Enterprise. Perseverance. Imagination.
☐ Exceptional　☐ Above Average　☐ Average　☐ Below Average　☐ Lacking

7. ENTHUSIASM
Interest in getting the job. Warmth. Sincerity
☐ Exceptional　☐ Above Average　☐ Average　☐ Below Average　☐ Lacking

8. GENERAL INTELLIGENCE
Imagination. Fertility of Ideas. Ability to Learn Easily. Ability to Apply Ideas and Knowledge Readily.
☐ Exceptional　☐ Above Average　☐ Average　☐ Below Average　☐ Unsatisfactory

9. LOGIC · COMMON SENSE
Mental Maturity. Reasoning and Conclusion. Dependability of Judgement.
☐ Exceptional　☐ Above Average　☐ Average　☐ Below Average　☐ Poor

10. ASPIRATIONS
☐ Aspires to top level position in management or profession.
☐ Satisfied to reach middle management or middle professional level.
☐ Prefers position of limited responsibility.
☐ Has not planned a long term career.

MILITARY SERVICE STATUS
☐ Veteran　☐ Draft Exempt　☐ Officer Candidate
☐ Draft Eligible　☐ In Reserve or Naitonal Guard　☐ Other

CATEGORY RANKING AND DEFINITIONS

Ranking 1 - Excellent	Very well prepared by past training and/or experience. High level of drive and maturity. Broad and balanced outlook. Very pleasant overall impression. Communicates very effectively and tactfully. Outstanding level of past achievements. Excellent potential.
Ranking 2 - Above Average	Well prepared by past training and experience. Good level of drive and maturity. Good flexible outlook. Quite pleasant general impression. Communicates quite effectively and tactfully. Excellent level of past achievements. Good Potential.
Ranking 3 - Average	Adequately prepared by past training and experience. Sufficient drive and maturity. Flexible outlook. Adequately pleasing general impression. Communicates with sufficient effectiveness and tact. Good in level of past achievements. Adequate potential.
Ranking 4 - Below Average	Marginal in adequacy of past training and/or experience. Some signs of drive and maturity. Some flexibility in outlook. No averse impressions. Communicates with some deficiencies. Fair in level of achievements. Limited potential.
Ranking 5 - Not Acceptable	Insufficiently prepared by past training and experience. Low level of drive and maturity. Rigid or poor outlook. Inappropriate general impressions. Serious communication difficulties. Extensive deficiencies in level of past achievements and attitudes.

INDICATE CATEGORY RANK FOR ALL GROUPS

INTERVIEW GROUPS

_____ ADMINISTRATIVE

Administrative Budget & Management Analysis 1
Educational Services Intern - Management
Educational Services Intern - Accounting
Management Intern
Personnel Technician
Trainee Management Information Specialist 2 - Programming
Trainee Management Information Specialist 2 - Systems analysis

_____ DATA COLLECTION & WRITING

Archivist 1
Curator 1
Publications Editor 1
Research Analyst 1 - General
Trainee - Student Admissions Examiner 2

_____ PUBLIC CONTACT

Labor Standards Representative 1
Manpower Specialist 1
Unemployment Compensation Analyst 1
Educational Services Intern - General
Public Information Officer 1
Trainee Right of Way Agent 1

_____ SOCIAL SERVICE

Disability Claims Adjudicator 1
Social Worker 1 - State
Social Worker 1 - County
Trainee Vocational Rehabilitation Counselor 2

_____ AREA SERVICES SPECIALIST 1 AND 2

_____
Signature

_____
Title

Item J

What If You're Third Best?

You have applied for a job. You have had your interview, and you feel that you rank third or fifth or ninth in qualifications. You may be right—and you may get the offer anyway. Here's why:

• The first candidate is making too much money, so the company's offer doesn't interest him.

• The second candidate lives in Florida and decides not to fight the northern winters.

• The third candidate is brilliant, but everybody in the company who met him decided that he's a jerk. They don't want him around.

• The fourth candidate lives in a distant city and is halfway through an MBA program, so he decides not to disrupt his educational program.

• The fifth candidate's spouse is making good money and wouldn't be able to find as good a job if they moved.

• The sixth candidate owns income property in his present city and decides against becoming an absentee landlord.

• The seventh candidate has just built a new house and the family loves it. They decide not to move.

• The eighth candidate has had five jobs in three years. The employer, concerned about his stability, passes.

You get the offer.

As number nine, you may be the best available. The job is just as good for you as it was for number one. If you hadn't applied or if you had let the competition discourage you, you wouldn't have received the offer.

14

RESUMES

How to make them and how to use them

Imagine your resume nestling in the middle of a stack of 200 resumes.

Picture a recruiter lugging the resumes home in a briefcase on Friday night. On Sunday afternoon, he opens a beer, flips on the TV Game of the Week, sits back in a comfortable chair, and attacks the pile of resumes. But he doesn't carefully scrutinize each resume. Instead, he really clips along, with one eye on the game and one on the resumes.

The average resume gets 10 seconds!

Do you think that's long enough for a major decision that can affect your life?

Not all recruiters are watching the Game of the Week as they zip through a stack of resumes, but recruiters do handle a lot of paper. Every day a recruiter for a big company will get a stack of mail two inches thick, made up almost totally of resumes, applications, and employment agency mailers. That makes for a 10-inch pile at the end of the week. In recent years, school districts have received as many as 500 resumes for one teaching job. That makes for a lot of boring reading.

Recruiters are busy people, and often the most your resume will get is a once-over-lightly look and a flick of the wrist into the rejection pile.

192

Again, consider a stack of 200 resumes. Then consider how you look on paper. Your resume might stop the recruiter, if it's a smashing one, with items such as these:

Education
Stanford University, Bachelor's Degree in Business.
Harvard University, Master's in Business Administration.
University of Chicago, one year postgraduate study in Economics.
Phi Beta Kappa

Experience
IBM Corporation, two years, sales.
US Department of Commerce, three years, assistant to the secretary.
Xerox Corp. one year sales, two years district sales manager.

Skills
Fluent in Russian, German, and Spanish.

Outside Activities
Teaching course in Economics at University of California–Berkeley.
Tournament bridge.
Fifth place in Boston Marathon.
Articles published in Harper's, Dunn's Review, Forbes Magazine.
Chairman of Governor's Commission on prisons.

Every name on that fictitous resume is prestigious, so most recruiters would probably want to talk to that "phenom." But most people's resumes aren't quite so impressive. Consider this background for a candidate for a high-level executive job:

Education
High school graduate.
Studied law at night school

Experience
Managed family farm for 11 years.
Worked as bank bookkeeper.
Was partner in clothing store.

Military
Was major in field artillery.
Colonel in Army Reserve.

Hobbies
Playing the piano.
Playing poker.

Not very impressive qualifications. The recruiter in front of the TV set might give that resume a glance, look up to see if the home team got a first down, and flip the resume into the "regret and file" stack. Yet the holder of those qualifications, Harry S. Truman, went on to get the biggest executive job of all.

The point is that people just do not come alive on paper. That's why I have continually stressed throughout this book that whenever possible you should make your first contact with the recruiter in person rather than through the mail. But when you do make your first contact in person, you should have your resume with you. And I do acknowledge that there are times when you will have to mail your resume in, such as when you answer a blind ad, or when it is impossible to travel to the employer's location.

When you send a resume, do it right. (See sample resume at the end of this chapter.) Here are some guidelines.

Production

Never, but **never,** send a hand-written resume. A typed resume, on high-quality bond paper, is the bare minimum.

Having your resume printed is a good investment. Find a good print shop. Select excellent paper. It should be white or off-white—no bold colors. A printed resume can be a nice plus, but it does have one weakness. It is not especially prepared for one particular employer. You do lose some of the personal touch when you send a printed resume, and you probably cannot tailor your printed resume to an individual employer or job.

Never send chintzy-looking reproductions. Don't send resumes that have been copied on inferior copying machines. Some copying machines turn out ugly copies on slippery, shiny paper. Others make copies that are hard to distinguish from originals. If you must reproduce your resume on a copying machine, use a good one.

When you type your resume, don't use a worn out ribbon. Don't send a resume that has strikeovers, words crossed out, or messy erasures.

Carefully proofread your resume (and any other correspondence you send to a potential employer). When you finish proofreading, give it to two other people to double-check and proofread. One additional proofreader is not enough. Too many people do not do a conscientious job of proofreading. Some people will quickly glance over your resume and say, "Looks good to me." And they'll miss three mistakes. Typing errors look sloppy. Spelling errors are fatal.

> **TIP:** Do not, in any correspondence with a potential employer, misspell "personnel." Personnel departments are flooded with correspondence addressed to the "Personal," "Personel," "Personnell," or "Personall" Department. If you do that, you are likely to be "rejekted."

Format

The layout of your resume should be clean and crisp. The resume is not a work of art, but is should be attractive to look at. It should not be a big gray block of type. Break it up. Skip a space between major items.

Very rarely should a resume be longer than two pages.

If your resume is one page, you can list your work experience chronologically. This order makes it easy for the reader to follow your career development. If it's two pages, you should list your work experience backwards, starting with your present job and working back. That way, your present job, which is probably the most important item in your work experience, won't be relegated to page 2. If it is on page 2, you may lose the reader before he ever gets to your big number.

Style

A resume needn't read like a novel. Sentences should be short and to the point. You don't even have to write complete sentences. Frangments will do. For example: "Sold supplies to dentists in three states. Worked six-day week."

Do not be pompous or wordy. Don't take 10 lines to describe one of your jobs when two lines are enough.

Content

Present everything you want the employer to know. That breaks down generally into four categories:

Personal Information

• Your name. Do not list yourself as Mr., Miss, Mrs., or Ms. Anyone who introduces himself as "Mr. Cunningham" sounds pompous. "Ms." will turn off a lot of employers. No need to do that; just list your first and last name.

If you are married and use your husband's last name, you should mention what your maiden name is so the potential employer can check any school transcripts or can check with any employers you worked for before you were married. You can do that by listing the name you use and saying parenthetically (maiden name was Maher).

• Age. Just list your age, not your date of birth. When you list only your date of birth, you force the recuiter to do some pesky arithmetic.

• Your address. Street address, apartment number if there is one, city, state, and zip code.

• Your phone number. Include the area code if you are applying for a job with a nonlocal organization or with a local organization that does business nationally. If the organization is strictly local, don't include the area code. Listing the area code could make the employer think your resume has been mass produced and is being sent to a lot of out-of-town employers.

• Marital status. A woman who is engaged need not list herself as engaged. She is single. Period. However, if you feel it is to your advantage to report that you are engaged, you certainly can do so. If your spouse's occupation would be an advantage to you in applying for the job, by all means say what your spouse does. If not, don't go into it.

• Children. If it's an advantage for you to list the number of children you have, go ahead. If not—if you're a woman with three young children—you might not want to list that information. Save it for the interview.

• Height and weight. There is usually no need to go into this tape measure stuff. If you're applying for a job as a basketball center and you're 7 feet 2 inches, list it.

• Military status. Some employers are definitely impressed if you are a veteran, so it's probably to your advantage to list your experience. If you were an officer or highly trained specialist, say so. Mention any special awards or commendations you received.

Education

Whether you went to college or not, you should list your high school. Maybe the recruiter went to the same school or has some special interest in the town where you went to high school. You never know what's going to interest someone.

In reporting on your education, you might want to carefully consider your strategy. If you graduated with a bachelor's degree in accounting and are applying for an accounting job, obviously you want to say that you majored in accounting. But if you are applying for a job in computer programming at an insurance company, and you majored in art (like the woman in chapter 13), you might not want to list your major. You can list your college, the year you graduated, and the fact that you received a bachelor's degree. If you list art as your major, the recruiter might say, "Why should we hire an art major to program computers?" But the same recruiter might be impressed by you in an interview. Remember, the woman in chapter 13 was hired on the basis of a good impression in an interview, not because of her resume.

If your grades in school were high, list them. If they were low, don't list them. Save it for the interview, when you will get a chance to explain low grades. If your overall grade point was 2.4 (A=4.0), but your grade point in your major was 3.7, list your grade point in your major—but be sure to make it clear that *is* your grade point in your major, not your overall grade point. Say, "Grade point in major was 3.7."

List any scholarships or academic awards you received.

If you are a new or recent graduate, emphasize school extracurricular activities. If you worked your way through school, say so. Employers are generally impressed by that.

Work Experience

Be thorough and succinct. List anything that would be significant in the job you are applying for. If you are applying for a supervisory job, emphasize any supervisory experience you have had. Tell how many people worked under you, what projects you directed, and what budgetary control you had.

Give the names of the places you worked at, the dates of your employment, and your duties. Emphasize promotions, special assignments, noteworthy accomplishments, and any professional awards you received. There is no need to list the reason you left. If you were fired, you don't have to say so on the resume.

Outside Activities and Interests

List any outside activity or skill that would make a good impression on the recruiter. Anything that shows community involvement, such as a charity drive chairmanship or service on a school board, is an asset.

It's probably safer to avoid listing political or ideological affiliations. Active membership in the Democratic or Republican Party probably should not be listed—the recruiter might be of the opposite stripe. If you're a member of the American Civil Liberties Union, the National Organization for Women, or the Young Americans for Freedom, you needn't scare the recruiter off by mentioning it. It's your private business. The same thing applies to the Masons and the Knights of Columbus. It would make no sense to give anyone who dislikes any of those organizations a chance to discriminate against you because of your affiliation.

List any significant publishing you have done, particularly in your field.

List any special accomplishments, such as patents, or excellence in some sport or intellectual activity.

You definitely should put forth the extra effort necessary to tailor the resume to the particular job or organization you're applying to.

There are several things you should avoid:

• Don't list career objectives on your resume. That narrows you down too much.

• Don't list references. Save that for later. You should say, however, on the resume or in a cover letter, that references will be furnished.

• Don't criticize previous bosses or organizations. You can, however, occasionally express a positive opinion. If an organization you now work for or worked for in the past is outstanding but little known, you can point out that it is an outstanding organization.

• Don't be a windbag. Some people go into laborious detail about their personal views, their professional attitudes, and their experience. Every recruiter occasionally gets a resume from someone who goes on for 20 pages about various phases of his life. One young man, about halfway through a 30-page resume, lapsed into a stream of consciousness and described his sexual encounter with a "tall, dark sylph" he met in the mountains.

Keep it businesslike.

Pictures

You should consider putting your picture on your resume. If you are an attractive man or woman, let your appearance work for you. Employers do consider such superficial things as whether you're good looking or not. If you are a nonwhite or if you are a woman applying for a traditionally male job or a man applying for a traditionally female job, you definitely should include your picture. It can make a big difference.

If you are having your resume printed, the printer can print the photo in the upper right corner of your resume. If you are not having your resume printed, you can clip your picture to your resume.

Applications

Most employers have standard application forms. You should fill them out neatly, and if possible, you should type. Again, proofread and double-check for errors.

Employers' applications have limitations. Often there is not enough space for you to elaborate on items you want to discuss at some length. You can shift the employer over to your turf, your resume, where you can say everything you want, *your* way. If you want to shift to your resume when you get to the work experience portion of the application, all you have to do is write "see resume" on that part of the application.

Cover Letters

Any time that you mail in a resume, you should send a cover letter along with it.

The cover letter should be brief and should follow standard business letter format (See example on page 203). The writing style should be semiformal, neither chatty nor stilted.

The cover letter is an excellent place to express your interest in the particular organization. You can include a paragraph or two on what impresses you about the organization and why you would like to work for it.

Cover letters should *always* be individualized—written exclusively to that one employer. Never send form letters.

The cover letter should include what job you are interested in, plus a few general comments about yourself.

I favor including in the cover letter either your present salary or the salary range you are interested in.

Many people disagree. They feel that if you include salary information it will knock you out of competition. I contend that if this information will knock you out early, it will knock you out later. If an employer has a job for $15,000, and you're making $18,000, the recruiter will not contact you because the company cannot afford you. What have you lost? Probably nothing. But maybe you've saved yourself some time. If you are making $12,500, the company with the $15,000 opening knows you are a candidate it can afford.

If you don't list salary information, the recruiter might pass on you simply because he won't gamble on the hassle. As a search consultant, I get many resumes and cover letters from high-level executives. Almost all of them report their salary in the letter.

The cover letter is another item where spending some money can pay off. Get some letterhead stationery and some matching envelopes printed.

When addressing your cover letter and the envelope, be absolutely certain that you have the name and title of the person to whom you are writing correct. If you have any doubt about the spelling of the name or about the title, call the personnel department of the organization and ask. The margin for error is enormous.

One of the cardinal rules of public relations is "Get that editor's name right." Public relations agents want to make a good impression on editors because they want editors to print their news releases in the paper. The name of the business editor of *The Milwaukee Journal* is Ross M. Dick. Over the years, news releases and other pieces of mail have been addressed to him with at least 80 variations of his name. Each time a new variation comes in, he clips it off the envelope and puts it on the ever-growing pile. Here are some samples of the way mail has been addressed to Ross M. Dick:

Mr. Roff Dick	Mr. Ross Dic
Mr. Ron Dick	Mr. Ross Dyck
Mr. Russ Dick	Mr. Ross Vick
Editor Ross Pick	Mr. Ross M. Dikk
Mr. Reece Dick	Mr. Nick Ross
Mr. Ross Dickey	Foss Dick
Mr. Soss Dick	Mr. Ralph Bick
Mr. Ralph Dick	Clarence M. Dick
Mr. Rosdick	Mr. Ross Diels
Ross Deih	Mr. Ross Wick
Mr. Oss Dick	Mr. Ross Duke
Mr. Rosa Dick	Mr. Richard Ross
Mr. Rolf Dick	Mr. Ross Kick
Mr. Ross Duck	Mr. Ross Emdick
Dick Rose, Esq.	Mr. Ross Click
Mr. Richard Rice	Mr. Ross Bick
Mr. Roth Dick	Mr. Ross Dich
Miss Rose M. Dick	Mr. Rossadick

With all that mail coming in, it's surprising that Mr. Dick remembers his own name.

Here's a sample resume for a woman who works for an advertising agency. She's answering an ad in a trade publication to be advertising manager for a sporting goods manufacturer in Dallas.

Resume

Ann Baker
Address: 6701 France Avenue South
Minneapolis, Minnesota 55419
Phone: 612-111-1111
Age: 28
Marital Status: Single

Education

High School: New Trier High School; Winnetka, Illinois.

College: University of Texas; graduated with bachelor of arts degree in 1969; had double major, English and political science; grade point was 3.5.

Part-time jobs while in college: Worked two years as file clerk in the Registrar's office. Wrote radio ads for Hi-Note Music Store, Austin, Texas.

Experience

Smear-On Cosmetics Corp., Los Angeles. From July of 1969 to August of 1972. Wrote ad copy for consumer accounts for radio, television, and magazines. Won two Los Angeles Advertising Club awards for television ads.

Smith, Jones & Brown Advertising Agency, Minneapolis. Started as senior copywriter in 1972. Wrote for all media. One account was a sporting goods store. In 1974 was promoted to account supervisor, in charge of two accounts—Buzz-Buzz Outboard Motors and Fluffy Bread.

Outside Interests

Sports—particularly tennis and racquetball
Painting
Photography

Here's a sample cover letter to accompany the resume of the woman applying for the advertising manager's job in Dallas.

Ann Baker
6701 France Avenue South
Minneapolis, Minnesota 55419

March 15, 1976

Mr. Jack King
Personnel Manager
XYZ Sporting Goods Corp.
1102 Pacific Avenue
Dallas, Texas 75202

Dear Mr. King:

I am highly interested in the job of advertising manager for XYZ.

My job at Smith, Jones & Brown has, for the last two years, involved considerable managerial responsibility.

I have enjoyed the managerial aspects of the job, and I am interested in a job with broader managerial duties. Your ad indicates that the job at XYZ is just what I have in mind.

I feel that it is important for an advertising person to like the product that is being plugged. I have always thought highly of XYZ equipment. My last two tennis racquets have been XYZ and I wouldn't get any other kind. Also, I'm impressed by the fact that XYZ golf clubs are widely considered to be the best on the market.

Furthermore, I like the Dallas area. I visited Dallas often when I was going to the University of Texas, and I always felt I would like to live there.

My present salary is $17,000. If you are interested in me for the job, I can furnish professional references.

I'll phone you at the end of the week and can answer any questions you might have.

Sincerely,

Ann Baker

Item K

Phone

You should regard the telephone as a tool for gathering information, *not for giving it out.*

The trouble is the recruiter feels the same way about the phone. He's not going to give out much information, and he certainly isn't going to make many positive commitments over the phone. The maximum commitment you can get over the phone is an appointment. But, as previous chapters have shown, you can lose your chances for an appointment by calling the recruiter. If you call in response to an ad or a tip, the recruiter can pry enough information out of you on the phone to tell you you don't qualify. Then you've ruined your chances for a later walk-in. You should not make initial contacts over the phone unless you absolutely cannot avoid it.

Sensible uses of the phone in the job hunting process include:

• Calling to find out the name of a company when an ad lists only a phone number. If the switchboard operator answers by telling the name of the company, you have the information. If not, ask whoever answers what company or employer it is. Then get off the line—don't get hustled into a phone interview.

• Calling to learn the name or job of the hiring decision maker.

• Calling a recruiter or a manager who has interviewed you to find out what's up. Don't call until the time the company official told you it would take to get back to you has expired.

• Frequent phone checks with employment agency counselors to learn what's going on and to make sure they don't forget about you. But don't overdo it; don't be a pest. Once every few days is sufficient.

Whenever you call an employer, be certain that there won't be a lot of commotion in the background on your end. You don't sound very professional when your voice is mingled with the sounds of squalling kids or a blaring television set. If you're calling from outside your house, pick a quiet spot. Don't call from a bar where loud rock music is playing on the juke box or from a highway where semis are rumbling past.

> **TIP:** *Never* call a potential employer collect, even when the employer suggests that you call collect. One student asked me if he should call collect to a company that was only 100 miles away. Only a clod does that. The cost of a long-distance phone call is at most a few dollars. Don't be a cheapskate when your career is involved.

15

SOME SPECIAL PEOPLE

Job hunting for women, older people, and minorities

I recently asked a recruiter to describe the best entry level candidate he ever interviewed. He answered: "It's impossible to single out any one. But ideally, that person would have unusual maturity, better than average grades and would be reasonably active in outside activities. In today's climate, being a black woman wouldn't hurt, either."

That statement sums up the state of the job market for many women and members of racial minorities. Or any other minority.

When you are a minority candidate applying for a job, you have leverage. Laws and guidelines are behind you. If you are a woman applying for a job in a traditionally male field or a man applying for a traditionally female job, the odds are that they will kick out the red carpet for you, particularly when the employer is a giant company.

It's no secret that plenty of corporations are scrambling to hire blacks, Latinos, and American Indians. Search consultants could store up fortunes just by filling employers' requests for candidates from racial minorities. The federal government is watching.

Companies are also under pressure to hire women, although the pressure to hire women is not as intense as it is to hire candidates from racial minorities.

This does not mean that any woman or candidate from a racial minority is a cinch to get a job, but it does mean that women and minority candidates can, in many cases, be choosier than white males.

While minority candidates do have some advantages, there is one trap: the pressure is for the government to *hire* minority group persons and women. There is less pressure to *promote* them.

There are still companies that would make you a window-dressing black or a token woman. They'll hire a few blacks (or women), pay them a decent salary, and put them in a visible position that has no growth potential.

And there are undoubtedly quite a few job candidates who wouldn't mind that. A woman on my campus asked me recently, "Do you know of anybody who's looking for a token woman?"

In the long run, however, it's unwise and demeaning to let them make a token out of you.

If you have long-term career objectives, you probably are much better off with an organization that has a solid history of hiring and promoting minority candidates than with an organization that is scurrying around to find some minority candidates because it is trying to land a government contract and wants to look good on paper.

So you should do whatever investigating you can. If you know someone who works for the company, ask him or her about the company's hiring and promoting history. You might want to ask the recruiter. Say, "Tell me the history of blacks in your company," or "What has been the history of women in your company?" or "What kind of jobs have they been promoted to?"

If you are militant, pull in your horns while you're try- ing to get a job. Employers are wary of someone who they fear will holler discrimination. And while they are in- terested in hiring women, they're afraid of feminists.

Recently a young woman who had graduated on my campus interviewed at an insurance agency. A couple of days later I ran into the two executives who interviewed her. They had been impressed. I knew her to be an ardent feminist, and I was expecting them to tell me that she had opened on them. But no. She had played it cool. And she got a job.

If you are a woman who objects to such customs as men opening doors for you or pulling your chair out in a restaurant, you should suppress your feelings during the hiring process. They're not going to like it if you bristle when a door is opened for you. On the other hand, they probably won't be impressed if you melt like butter. Try to strike a happy medium. If someone opens a door or offers you a light, simply treat it as a common courtesy extended by one considerate person to another. In other words, keep it businesslike.

The 1975 *Endicott Report* published the results of an inquiry into the hiring of women graduates.

A total of 145 companies reported that they hired 2,484 women graduates from 1975 classes. From 1976 classes, a total of 164 companies hope to hire at least 3,620 college women, an increase of 45 percent.

Respondents were asked this question: "What can college women do to make themselves more employable in your company?" Here are the most frequently mentioned suggestions by employers.

Illustrative comments include the following:

> "Get into the mainstream of disciplines from which employers now hire most graduates — business and engineering."
>
> "Take more business-related and technical courses. Get away from courses and degrees that have traditional female dominance."
>
> "Tell other women to go into engineering."
>
> "Major in accounting, obtain good grades, demonstrate leadership ability, and show enthusiasm for our work."
>
> "Learn about opportunities available to them. Be flexible about assignments."

Number of Companies	Response
42	Take technical courses. Go into engineering.
35	Take business-related courses (accounting, business administration, computer science, economics, and finance).
28	Get experience in business (summer employment, part-time jobs, co-op or work-study programs).
18	Develop more definite career plans. Clarify objectives. Secure vocational counseling.
12	Acquire better understanding of business, knowledge of entry level jobs.
7	Be more flexible; be willing to travel; be willing to relocate.
5	Work more closely with placement offices. Get on interview schedules.
4	Start in smaller companies.

"Be *really* open to relocation. More clearly defined career goals."

"Demonstrate that they can adjust to work in a business environment."

"Get work experience so that they have confidence in their abilities and can show commitment to a career."

"Be willing to live in small towns where our plants are."

"They are as employable as males."

The 1975 *Endicott Report* has this to say about the employment of graduates who are black.

It was reported by 109 companies that a total of 1,513 black graduates were employed from 1975 classes. From 1976 classes, at least 2,194 black graduates will be hired by 152 companies. This is an increase of 45 percent.

When employers were asked what black graduates can do to make themselves more employable in their companies, the following suggestions were most frequently mentioned. (Some employers indicated that suggestions were the same as for women.)

Illustrative comments include the following:

"Obtain more business-related experience. Participate in more college activities. Use the

Number of Companies	Response
40	Study engineering and technical subjects including mathematics and science.
33	Take business-related courses, such as accounting, business administration, and computer science.
16	Have clearer career goals and objectives.
15	Get work experience in business through summer employment, part-time jobs, or in co-op or work-study programs.
12	Be better prepared for interview. Improve interviewing technique.
6	Be academically competitive. Get good grades.
5	Improve self-confidence.
4	Utilize placement services on campus. Get on interview schedules.

placement office. Prepare better for interviews."

"Better understanding of the business community and how it operates."

"Emphasize engineering and accounting
courses in their curriculum."

"We need to have more blacks with accounting majors."

"Continue emphasis on improving math and
English skills."

"Black cultural courses are fine, but they do
not prepare them for business."

"Take more demanding and business-
oriented courses."

"Many black graduates would be more employable with stronger academic backgrounds."

"There are almost no black graduates with
training or interest in our field, power engineering."

"Evaluate and match personal qualities
with possible career opportunities.

"Our home office is in a small Midwest town,
and it is hard to get them to move up here."

"More should sign up for interviews. Apply!"

Changing Jobs

Don't leap onto the job market without carefully assessing your present situation. A lot of people jump too fast
and land in a mess.

Any job gets boring after a while.

If you're bored, don't look around without first talking
to your present supervisors. Maybe they will find something more interesting for you. If money is your problem,
ask for a raise. The worst they can do is say no.

A word of caution on threats to quit: don't threaten
unless you mean it. They might take you up on it.

212

A technical supervisor at one company was constantly grousing about conditions. He'd say, "If I don't get more work space, I'm getting out of here," or "Unless we get another secretary, you're not going to see me around here anymore." He tried it once too often. After one such threat, his boss extended his hand for a handshake and said, "Bring your letter of resignation in in 15 minutes. I hope you find something good." It took the man three months to find another job.

Another dangerous game is to try to use another job offer that you don't want to accept as leverage for more money or a promotion from your present employer. Again, they might call your bluff. If you are secure in your job, however, it doesn't hurt to tell your present boss that you got a job offer *if you make it absolutely clear that you're not going to take it.* You can say something like, "I'm not going to take it, but the XYZ Company offered me a job at $27,000 a year."

It doesn't hurt to let them know somebody else loves you.

One of the most important steps in changing jobs is quitting your present job.

The quitting process actually begins when you start looking for a new job. Don't tell your present bosses or people you are working with, even if you're just looking around to see what jobs are out there. If your superiors find out about it, they might start to think of you as a lame duck. This could mean that they will give someone else the raise they might have given you or give to others choice assignments that might have gone to you. And that's only logical. There is little incentive to keep you happy. So keep quiet.

In the previous section, I advised anyone who is unhappy with his or her present job to go to the boss and see if something can be done to improve the situation. But I strongly advise that you don't include in that discussion the hint that unless something is done you'll quit.

Many supervisors will say to their most valued subordinates, "If things ever get to the point where you are thinking of quitting, I want you to tell me first and I will either fix the problem or help you find your new job." Bosses make this offer in good faith. But it rarely works out the way you'd like it to. And there are reasons. Sometimes the boss can't fix you up. Then because of budget or organizational problems, you might want to start looking.

When you get your new job, I suggest that you resign in a confidential manner, in writing. You can write a letter to your boss similar to this:

Dear Boss:

I have accepted a job with the ABC Company, so I am submitting my resignation effective March 15.

I will treat this information as confidential until it's released by your office. I have enjoyed my experiences here, and I wish you and the company well in the future.

Sincerely,

The resignation should be temporarily confidential because the boss might not want anyone else to know about it yet. He might want to feel out some people, either inside or outside the company, about your job. He may have other problems you don't know about. So give him operating room by keeping your mouth shut until he announces that you are quitting. Such consideration for your boss might result in better references for you in the future.

Older Candidates

Not too many years ago, anyone over 40 could expect to have a tough time in the job market. These days the walls don't fall in on people until about the age of 50.

But the wise person doesn't let the walls fall in. The same principles that apply to anyone else apply to job seekers over 50. The brisk, alert candidate who can make a solid contribution to an organization has a lot of advantages: maturity, experience, stability. You should make those strong points work for you. Point out the depth of your experience; emphasize that you're no risk to the potential employer. If you have a solid work record, play it up. It's a strong selling point.

The major obstacle you might have to overcome is a feeling on the part of some employers that your work habits are so firmly entrenched that you aren't flexible enough to adapt to their system. Emphasize that you are flexible. Give examples of how you can adapt.

You might also be questioned about your health. If you have a health problem, be honest about it. But stress that you are still able to perform the job effectively.

Image is extremely important for the older job seeker. Two facets of image deserve special attention:

• Aggressiveness. You might not want to be as aggressive as the younger job seeker, particularly if you are dealing with a young recruiter or manager. While aggressiveness might be attractive in a younger candidate, a young recruiter might interpret a 61-year-old's aggressiveness as crochetiness.

• Be brisk. Be sure to present yourself as a vigorous, lively person. As a search consultant, I frequently have called prospects who have answered the phone with the enthusiasm of a mackerel: "Heeeellllllooo."

I have heard telephone greetings so faint, so drowsy, and so lifeless that, even though it was only seven in the evening, I have said, "I hope I didn't wake you." And the drowsy reply is, "Nooo, I haven't gone to bed yet."

I scrawl on the data sheet in front of me "Tired Old Man." And in a very short time, I end the conversation.

Be alive.

Fresh Out of High School

New high school graduates think they're competing with other new graduates when they go out to look for a job. Wrong. They're up against everyone in the field. Any high school graduate applying for a job as a mechanic, clerk, secretary, welder, construction worker, bank teller, truck driver or anything else is likely to be competing with people who have 2, 10, and 20 years of experience.

Here's why. A lot of those jobs pay the same rate to beginners that they pay for people who have been at it for years. Union contracts frequently require that every union employee will be at maximum pay after 60 days.

When a recruiter in a manufacturing company looks out in the waiting room and sees a fresh-faced, 18-year-old high school graduate and a 27-year-old married guy who looks as though he knows what to do with a welding torch, he's probably going to be prejudiced toward the older man. The older man is a known quantity. He has experience, and he might be established in the community with kids and a mortgage.

But if you are the 18-year-old, don't be scared off. The solid-looking 27-year-old might have been fired from his last three jobs. He might have two divorces behind him and a couple of drunken driving arrests on his record.

You have some good things going for you. The recruiter knows that you probably haven't developed any bad work habits yet. He figures that you probably have the eagerness of youth and that you might be more flexible in the work assignments you will accept without grousing. Furthermore, companies like to keep a steady stream of young people pouring in. They don't want their work force to age all at once.

The recruiter knows, too, that you might have ambitions of some day being a superintendent and that you'll work hard to realize those ambitions. He knows that the 40-year-old candidate he talked to yesterday won't be a superintendent. That candidate has been in the work force for 20 years and hasn't done any supervising. But you are a challenging unknown. Recruiters often ask new high school graduates, "Do you have any interest in getting into management some day?" They don't ask 40-year-old candidates that question.

Despite those advantages, you still are an underdog. When you apply for your first job out of high school, you are as close to going in hat in hand and saying "Please give me a job" as you will ever be in your life. That is because you have nothing to sell. You probably have never had a full-time job before, so you're not able to say, "I worked there for four years and never missed a day." (Although it does help to be able to point to an outstanding attendance record in school.)

What you have to do in the interview is capitalize on your advantages. Exploit the recruiter's positive expectations as to what an 18-year-old should be: eager, ambitious, responsive, and highly trainable.

You can convince him that you're eager by simply telling him that you want the job and that you're anxious to demonstrate what you're capable of doing. You can convince him you're ambitious by telling him that while you don't know much about the business world yet, yes, you would like to advance. If you are taking or are planning to take courses at a local college or technical school, tell the recruiter. Any indication that you want to further your knowledge and skills will impress the recruiter. A candidate for a secretarial job who is taking bookkeeping, accounting, finance, or any course that has to do with the written word, such as English literature or composition, will score a plus with the recruiter. A candidate for a job as a department store clerk who is taking merchandising, bookkeeping, or a salesmanship course should tell the recruiter about it.

There are two other chords that a new high school graduate must hit with the recruiter — maturity and respectfulness.

You can show your maturity by your appearance. Avoid wild fashions. Your clothes should be simple and conservative. The biggest mistake women just out of high school

make is trying to sex it with their clothes and mannerisms. It doesn't work.

If you are applying for a job as a laborer, you're obviously not going to show up in a business suit. You probably will wear denim or khaki pants. They should be
spotless. It helps if they're new. Then they have a clean,
starchy look to them. Wear a clean sweater, shirt, or
blouse to the interview. Don't wear sweatshirts; they look
sloppy. You can wear work shoes, but make sure they're
not broken down or dirty.

The appearance of someone looking for a job in a factory is every bit as important as the appearance of someone applying for an executive job. The same principles
are operating. Look at it from the recruiter's point of
view. There are two candidates in the lobby. One has an
immaculate pair of pants and a clean shirt. The other has
a greasy pair of overalls and a grubby T-shirt. Which one
is the recruiter going to think is the more dependable,
careful, and tidy worker?

If you are applying for a job in an office, bank, or department store, you should case the place in advance to
see how the people dress.

To further your image of maturity, your manner should
be reserved and dignified. That does not mean one- and
two-word answers to the recruiter's questions, but it does
mean that you should speak in a modulated voice and
that you shouldn't babble. Steer clear of "in talk." High
school expressions irritate adults. I always advise new
high school graduates not to make *any* attempt at humor
in a job interview. Eighteen-year-old humor can rattle
forty-year-old nerves.

Convincing the recruiter that you are respectful is extremely important. The image of youth has changed in
the last 20 years. In the 1950s and before, adults took the
respect of young people for granted. They considered
young people impressionable, pliable, and manageable.
And that, generally, was what young people were like.

Then in the 1960s, with the protest movement and the youth rebellion, young people developed a new image. People over 30 began to think of youth as a snarling, malcontented dragon trying to knock down all their systems and devour them.

That turbulent era has passed, but the image lingers. Plenty of adults in the establishment still view youths with fear, dislike, and suspicion. They still feel that young people are a hostile force, with alien values, lifestyles, and mannerisms. You should work this widespread prejudice to your advantage. Adults who carry a bitter anti-youth taste in their mouths from the 1960s are highly impressed by any 18-year-old who makes them think, "What a nice young man," or "What a polite young woman." Your attitude in job interviews should be calculated to make recruiters and managers think just that of you.

Being extremely pleasant is a good start.

Calling the recruiter "sir" or "ma'am" will help. When older candidates use "sir" or "ma'am" extensively, they come off as subservient or ridiculous. An 18-year-old candidate who uses "sir" or "ma'am" comes off as someone who is "not like the rest of those punks."

Part Time

Applying for part-time work involves all the principles that are involved in applying for full-time work. There is one major difference. A high percentage of part-time and summer employees are hired for political reasons. Trade-offs are frequent.

The recruiter for Company A will call the recruiter for Company B and say, "Can you find a summer spot for our president's son? He's a sophomore in engineering." And the recruiter for Company B will say, "Yes, I think we can find something for him in the lab. Can you find something for the daughter of our vice-president of finance?" And the other recruiter says, "Sure." Both jobs are probably created.

Your father or mother doesn't have to be an executive for you to get a good part-time job in a company. Students whose parents work in the shop always have an advantage over outsiders with no connections. If you have pull, use it.

If you're looking for a summer job, start early. For some jobs, January isn't too soon to apply. May is usually too late.

Item L

Reference

Nobody gives a potential employer a negative reference letter. Or even one that's lukewarm. Employers know this. Because the candidate will show a potential employer only rave reviews, the employer doesn't pay much attention to such letters.

Even references you list on applications or resumes aren't checked as thoroughly as they used to be. Employers know they are probably being steered to somebody who will thump the tub for you. But sometimes an employer *will* phone check your references, so be sure you have set them up. Ask permission of anyone you want to list as a reference. Then, your recommender will not be taken by surprise when the employer calls and will have a spiel prepared about how you can leap tall buildings at a single bound.

Give only professional references — people who have worked with you. Previous bosses are best. Pals, neighbors, tennis-playing cronies are worthless.

Most employers who come to my campus do not ask faculty members for references on students. But, again, some do. So a student ought to get in tight with at least one faculty member by the junior year. You don't have to be covert about what you're doing. You don't have to hang around the prof, merely browning him up in hopes that he notices you.

Come right out and tell him why you want to get to know him. Tell him, "Next year I would like to have a reference from a faculty member, and I am hoping it will be you. I realize you don't know me yet, but one of the things I want to do this semester is to make sure that you get to know me." Then stop in his office once in a while. Join him for lunch some day. Make sure that he will be able to comment on more than your class work. Get to know him well enough so that he can tell a potential employer about your personality, your goals, and your maturity.

A lot of students make the mistake of listing as references faculty members who hardly know them. Then when the employer calls, the faculty member might say, "Who the hell is he?" or "Oh, yes, I think I had her in a class two years ago." The employer is going to think you're not too swift.

The area where references count the most on campus is education. School districts check out potential teachers. They query education faculty members and look into critiques on a candidate's practice teaching.

References can also be important in fields involving talent — dance, theater, journalism, art.

> **CAUTION:** There are several circumstances in which you might not want potential employers to check your references until you are at some advanced stage in the hiring process. You probably wouldn't want a current employer to know you are looking. You might have contacted 10 or 15 organizations about a job, and you don't want all of them bugging your references. If you don't want your references checked before you have had one or two interviews with a company, don't list your references on your resume. If it doesn't matter to you, go ahead and list them.